THE BEST-KEPT SECRET TO IMPROVED BANKING PROFITS

THE BEST-KEPT SECRET TO IMPROVED BANK PROFITS

The Ultimate Banker's Guide to Making More Money, Doing Fewer Deals and Taking Less Risk That 99% of Bankers Aren't Doing Today.

GREG O'DONNELL

"America's Leading Authority on Guaranteed Lending Programs"

TFC PRESS

O'Fallon, Missouri

Copyright © 2013 Greg O'Donnell

All rights reserved. No portion of this book may be reproduced mechanically, electronically, or by any other means, including photocopying, without written permission of the publisher. It is illegal to copy this book, post it to a website, or distribute it by any other means without permission from the publisher.

Cover and Interior Design: Imagine! Studios, LLC
www.ArtsImagine.com

Published by TFC Press
O'Fallon, Missouri

ISBN 13: 978-1-937545-03-1
Library of Congress Control Number: 2013935115

Second TFC Press printing: May 2013

"The world is my country, all mankind are my brethren, and to do good is my religion."

THOMAS PAINE

TABLE OF CONTENTS

Chapter 1
INTRODUCTION—WHY I WROTE THIS BOOK 1

Chapter 2
NOT JUST FOR FARMERS AND RANCHERS 5

Chapter 3
IT'S ALL ABOUT PERCEPTION 15
    Section 1: Bank Board and Management *15*
    Section 2: Regulators and Loan Policies *21*
    Section 3: Customers *24*

Chapter 4
YOUR BEST MARKETING OPPORTUNITIES
AND HOW TO REACH THEM 27

Chapter 5
UNIQUE LENDING OPPORTUNITIES THAT
BENEFIT YOUR COMMUNITY 31

Chapter 6
THE SECONDARY MARKET 35

Chapter 7
THE COACHING PROGRAM 45

Bonus 1
BASIC STEPS FOR PROCESSING A USDA B&I
GUARANTEED LOAN............................. 49

Bonus 2
BANK BOARD PRESENTATION.................... 63

Appendix A
USDA BUSINESS AND INDUSTRY GUARANTEED
LOAN PROGRAM................................. 65

Appendix B
USDA COMMUNITY FACILITIES GUARANTEED
LOAN PROGRAM................................. 99

Appendix C
USDA GUARANTEED LOAN PROGRAM
DEFAULT, PROTECTIVE ADVANCES, AND
LIQUIDATION REGULATION 121

Appendix D
RD 1980-41 125

Appendix E
SAMPLE OF FARMERMACII, LLC SECONDARY
MARKET FOR USDA GUARANTEED LOANS
WEEKLY RATE LINE............................ 127

Appendix F
B&I AND CF INFORMATION CHECKLIST......... 129

Appendix G
B&I AND CF SAMPLE TABLE OF CONTENTS..... 131

Appendix H
GUIDELINE FOR FINANCIAL FEASIBILITY 135

Appendix I
CONDITIONAL COMMITMENT.................. 139

Appendix J
LOAN NOTE GUARANTEE 141

Appendix K
RD AN 4483 BUSINESS AND INDUSTRY GUARANTEED LOAN AND SECTION 9007 RURAL ENERGY FOR AMERICA PROGRAMS LENDER FINANCIAL ANALYSIS REQUIREMENTS.......... 145

ABOUT THE AUTHOR 151

Chapter 1

INTRODUCTION—WHY I WROTE THIS BOOK

RICHARD BRANSON, THE founder of Virgin Group, said, "For me, building a business is all about doing something to be proud of, bringing talented people together, and creating something that's going to make a difference to other people's lives."

Over the past eighteen years, I have quietly made a huge difference in many people's lives through work originating and placing government guaranteed loans throughout the United States. I have seen the benefits to individuals, communities, and bank shareholders that come from using little-known and extremely valuable loan programs provided by the United States Department of Agriculture (USDA). As a leading authority in using the Business and Industry (B&I) and Community Facilities (CF) loan programs, I am now turning my attention toward making these programs better known while helping bankers across the country use them to improve their communities and increase their banks' bottom lines. I wrote this book to bring talented people together to make a difference in more people's lives.

Through my coaching program, I am working with bankers like you to strengthen communities using resources that are available, attractive, legal, profitable, and low risk.

BEGIN USING THE PROGRAMS THE COMPTROLLER OF THE CURRENCY RECOMMENDS

I want to make it perfectly clear that I am not writing this book as a banker. I don't pretend to be a banker, and I don't try to make anybody believe I'm a banker. I have not written this book to teach anything about banking. Rather, I've written this book to show bankers how to do fewer deals, make more money, take less risk, and use strategies that the comptroller of the currency suggests banks should be using to increase their bottom line.

My business has grown solely from referrals and repeat business. The only way I have been able to do this is by giving my clients true value for the fee they pay. The first question that always arises when I talk with bankers is, "If this is such a great deal, why isn't every bank doing it?" There is one simple answer: Most banks don't know about it, or they have misconceptions or misunderstandings about the programs. The fact is that the USDA does not market these lending programs very aggressively, so they are often underutilized. That's the first reason I wrote this book: The USDA doesn't promote these programs, so I decided that I would. They are just too good to ignore.

The second reason I wrote this book is to share the knowledge I've gained over the past eighteen years. My goal is to make it easy and satisfying for more bankers to do more of these deals. I know all of the questions and objections, so throughout the book I will bring them up and then answer them. Knowledge of these programs creates a competitive advantage for you and your bank. From my experience, clients who think outside the box and use these programs don't talk about them with their competition. In fact, they keep this knowledge as a closely guarded secret. One of our coaching clients with about $190 million in assets made more than $3 million from guaranteed lending in recent years. Their return on assets (ROA) is more than 3 percent. Their banking buddies watch the Call Reports and wonder what they are doing. This book outlines some of the strategies they've used to become more profitable.

The third reason I wrote this book is to multiply our efforts to make a difference in people's lives by expanding the number of bankers who discover and embrace the secrets I share in this book. Imagine helping your community build a new Critical Access Hospital, a kidney dialysis center, or a telemedicine center. Imagine expanding your role as your community's banker to lift the economic vitality of your community—with low risk and higher profits. Everybody wins!

The best answer to the question, "Why isn't everybody doing it?" is because they don't know what they don't know.

COULD THIS BE YOUR BANK'S "ACRES OF DIAMONDS"?

The story is now famous due to the teaching of Russell Conwell and the late Earl Nightingale. The story has it that a farmer in Africa heard of all the great and glorious fields of diamonds being discovered throughout the continent. He decided he would seek his own fortune and hunt for diamonds. Selling his farm, the farmer went out and searched for years, to no avail. He finally killed himself by jumping in a river. Meanwhile, back on his farm, the farmer who bought the land was walking through the creek and found a large stone that looked rather interesting and placed it on his mantel. A friend noticed the rock one day and asked the farmer if he knew what he had found. Puzzled, the farmer responded no. The friend then informed him it was a diamond, possibly one of the largest ever found. The astonished farmer went on to say the creek was littered with stones just like this one, maybe not as big, but they were in abundant supply. The farm the first farmer had sold to search for "acres of diamonds" turned out to be the biggest diamond mind in Africa.

The question bears asking: Could the USDA programs and the lending opportunities in your backyard possibly be your "acres of diamonds"?

From personal experience with the other banks I've worked with I will tell you the answer is YES! Join me today as we uncover your acres of diamonds.

In this book I have included three very valuable bonus sections that I believe you will not find anywhere else. In the first bonus section are the basic steps to follow in processing a USDA guaranteed loan. This section walks you through each step of the process from packaging through servicing these loans. The second bonus section is a completely generic presentation to the bank's management team or board of directors, showing them the benefits of the USDA guaranteed loan programs. And third, we have provided a comparison of the USDA guaranteed loan program with the Small Business Administration (SBA) 7(a) loan program.

Chapter 2

NOT JUST FOR FARMERS AND RANCHERS

THE BUSINESS AND Industry (B&I) and Community Facilities (CF) programs offered through the Rural Development division of the U.S. Department of Agriculture (USDA) are either completely unfamiliar to most in the United States, or bankers who have heard of them think they apply only to farmers and ranchers. On the contrary, the USDA guarantees loans made by eligible lenders to rural businesses as a credit enhancement, to assist lenders with risk mitigation and capital management. Rural Development's mission is to increase economic opportunity and improve the quality of life for all rural Americans.

Most banks in the United States could utilize these programs in one way or another. Below is a quick overview of both programs (for details, see Appendices A and B).

BUSINESS AND INDUSTRY (B&I) GUARANTEED LOAN PROGRAM

The B&I program can apply to almost any business located in rural America. A borrower may be a cooperative organization, corporation, partnership, or other legal entity organized and operated on a profit or nonprofit basis; an Indian tribe on a federal or state reservation or other federally recognized tribal group; a public body; or an individual. Individual borrowers must be citizens of the United States or reside in the United States after being legally admitted for permanent residence. Corporations or other nonpublic organization borrowers must be at least 51 percent owned by persons who are either citizens of the United States or reside in the United States after being legally admitted for permanent residence.

WHAT ENTERPRISES QUALIFY FOR USDA FUNDING?

It is actually easier to list enterprises that do not qualify for the program: farms, ranches, golf courses, gambling, illegal business activities, or lines of credit. The government offers four pages describing all eligible projects and two pages describing ineligible projects (see Appendices A and B).

EXAMPLES OF B&I PROJECTS THAT WOULD QUALIFY FOR USDA FUNDING (CHART 1)

Manufacturing Plants	Textile Manufacturers
Processing Plants	Pre-Fab Buildings
Distribution Depots	Wholesale operations
Retail Operations	Strip Centers
Yarn Texturizers	Hotels and Motels
Antique Malls	Restaurants

Rodeo Arenas	Warehouses
Guest Ranches	Fitness Centers
Marina Operations	Tourist/Recreation Facilities
Cellular Towers	Vending Companies
Physical Therapy Facilities	Gas Pipelines
Senior Living Facilities	Family Entertainment Facilities
Child Care Facilities	Nursing Homes
Assisted Living Centers	Convenience Stores
Medical Office Buildings	Dental Offices
Veterinarian Hospitals	Oil Refineries
Cold Storage Facilities	Bottled Water Companies
Auto Dealerships	Car Wash Facilities
Lumber Mills	Franchises
Truck Stops	Mulch Manufacturing
Fruit Processing	Coal Mines
Equipment Dealers	Health Care Facilities
Agricultural Processing	

EXAMPLES OF B&I PROJECTS THAT WOULD NOT QUALIFY FOR USDA FUNDING (CHART 2)

Agricultural	Charitable Institutions
Golf Courses	Churches
Prostitution[1]	Church Controlled Organizations
Gambling Facilities	Fraternal Organizations
Illegal Activities	Lending Institutions
Investment Institutions	Insurance Companies
Racetracks	Casinos

---

1 We suppose this is specifically stated in the regulations because someone actually utilized the program where prostitution was legal which probably would not be the best publicity for the agency.

The borrower must be engaged in or propose to engage in a business that will do one or more of the following:

- Provide employment

- Improve the economic or environmental climate

- Promote the conservation, development, and use of water for aquaculture

- Reduce reliance on nonrenewable energy resources by encouraging the development and construction of solar energy systems and other renewable energy systems.

B&I loans are normally available in rural areas, which include all areas other than cities or towns of more than 50,000 people, and the contiguous and adjacent urbanized area of such cities or towns. You can always confirm any question about the eligibility of specific locations with your regional or state USDA office. I recommend checking with the USDA, as on occasion I have seen an ineligible business across the street or road from an eligible business.

I must warn you, however, that in some cases the local offices give the wrong information. As the leading authority on the USDA guaranteed loan programs I've personally had numerous situations in which the banks have been told that the business or project wouldn't qualify due to its location, but, armed with the correct information, I've spoken to the local offices and helped them to realize the project does indeed qualify for a USDA loan guarantee. As one banking friend said, "Greg, you know these rules better that the people working in the USDA offices!" That may well be true, but I will say that it helps having eighteen years in the business solely focused on these USDA loan programs.

WHAT CAN THE LOANS BE USED FOR?

Loan purposes must be consistent with the general purpose contained in the regulation. Examples include, but are not limited to, the following:

- Business and industrial acquisitions when the loan will keep the business from closing, prevent the loss of employment opportunities, or provide expanded job opportunities

- Business conversion, enlargement, repair modernization, or development

- Purchase and development of land, easements, right-of-way, buildings, or facilities

- Purchase of equipment, leasehold improvement, machinery, supplies, or inventory

The percentage of guarantee, up to the maximum allowed, is a matter of negotiation between the lender and the agency. The maximum percentage of guarantee is 80 percent for loans of $5 million or less, 70 percent for loans between $5 million and $10 million, and 60 percent for loans exceeding $10 million. I have found that the maximum guarantee is easy to negotiate with the USDA.

The total amount of agency loans to one borrower must not exceed $10 million. However, under certain circumstances, at the administrator's discretion, the administrator may grant an exception to the $10 million limit for loans of $25 million. Some of these larger projects historically have included ethanol plants that have not been that successful.

The maximum loan terms for real estate may not exceed thirty years. Machinery and equipment repayment may not exceed the useful life of the machinery and equipment purchased with loan funds or fifteen years, whichever is less. Working capital repayment may not exceed seven years.

WHAT ARE THE TERMS AND COLLATERAL REQUIRED?

The lender and applicant negotiate the interest rate for the guaranteed loan; it may be either fixed or variable, as long as it is a legal rate. The variable interest rate may be adjusted at different intervals (not more often than quarterly) during the term of the loan.

The appraised collateral value must be documented to show that it is sufficient to protect the interest of the lender and the agency. The discounted collateral's appraised/booked value is normally at least equal to the loan amount, which is consistent with bank policy.

Normal Discounting:

- Real Estate—80 percent of appraised value
- Equipment—75 percent of cost or appraised value
- Accounts Receivable—80 percent of receivables less than ninety days
- Inventory—50 percent of cost

COMMUNITY FACILITIES (CF) GUARANTEED LOAN PROGRAM

The Community Facilities (CF) guaranteed loan program assists lenders in developing essential community facilities in rural areas and towns of up to 20,000 in population. Please note here that the CF program does not have the same contiguous or adjacent restrictions as the B&I regulations. This means that some smaller suburbs that may not qualify for the B&I program could possibly qualify for the CF program. It is a good idea to confirm specific locations with your regional or state USDA office. Loans are available to public entities such as municipalities, counties, and special-purpose districts, as well as to nonprofit corporations and tribal governments.

COMMUNITY FACILITIES TYPICALLY FUNDED UNDER THE CF GUARANTEED LOAN PROGRAM (CHART 2)

- Community health services, such as health clinics, assisted-living facilities, and hospitals
- Fire, rescue, and public-safety facilities, such as police cars, fire trucks, and police stations
- Educational and cultural facilities, such as schools, libraries, and theaters
- Transportation facilities, such as airports, street improvements, or bus service
- Community support services, such as child or adult day care
- Public buildings and improvements, including community and multipurpose centers.

Applicants must have the legal authority to borrow and repay loans, to pledge security for loans, and to construct, operate, and maintain the facilities. They must also be financially sound and able to organize and manage the facility effectively.

Loans may be used to construct, enlarge, or improve community facilities for health care, public safety, and public services. This can include costs to acquire land needed for a facility, pay necessary professional fees, and purchase equipment required for its operation.

Feasibility studies are normally required when loans are for start-up facilities, or for existing facilities when the project will significantly change the borrower's financial operations.

Refinancing for existing debts may be eligible for a CF loan if the debt being refinanced is a secondary part of the loan, is associated with the project facility, and the applicant's creditors are unwilling to extend or modify existing terms.

The interest rates for guaranteed loans, determined by the lender and borrower, may be fixed or variable. The program guarantees up to 90 percent of any loss of interest or principal on the loan, up to $40 million.

Repayment of the loan must be based on tax assessments, revenues, fees, or other sources of money sufficient for operation and maintenance, reserves, and debt retirement. Loan repayment terms may not exceed the applicant's authority (under state law or organizational structure), the useful life of the facility, or a maximum of forty years.

IS OUR BANK TOO SMALL TO DO THESE KINDS OF PROJECTS?

The USDA guaranteed loan programs were designed to assist smaller banks in making larger loans, because only the nonguaranteed portion of the loan counts against the bank's legal lending limit.

BANK BENEFITS FROM PARTICIPATION IN THE B&I AND CF PROGRAMS

- The federally guaranteed portion of the loan is protected against loss, reducing lenders' credit risk exposure.

- There is an active secondary market for guaranteed loans. This secondary market includes brokers like Banes Capital and Coastal Securities, as well as direct buyers, including other banks, insurance companies, and even some agriculture banks. The secondary market is robust because these loans carry the full faith and credit of the U.S. Government. These guarantees are traded like any U. S. Treasury notes or government paper, providing lenders with liquidity options. This secondary market allows banks to instantly profit from the loans by selling the guaranteed portion to other investors and reap premiums at closing of the loan. This is discussed further in Chapter 6.

- Lenders have the flexibility to use their own forms, loan documents, and security instruments.

- The guaranteed portion of the loan does not count against bank lending limits.

- Guaranteed loans may be considered to satisfy Community Reinvestment Act (CRA) requirements.

Source: Comptroller of the Currency, Administrator of National Bank, US Department of the Treasury Community Development

14 THE BEST-KEPT SECRET TO IMPROVED BANKING PROFITS

Request The CD "The Best Kept Secret to Improved Banking Profits" by going to **www.TheUSDALoanCoach.com**

Normally $49, this CD is free of charge to readers of this book!

Chapter 3

IT'S ALL ABOUT PERCEPTION

SECTION 1: BANK BOARD AND MANAGEMENT

GUARANTEED LENDING IS exactly what each bank makes it. One of my first interviews for this book was with a longtime Tulsa, Oklahoma, banker who is currently CEO of his bank, which has total assets in excess of $300 million. I had done a few loans with him at other banks he had owned and sold. It had been more than ten years since we had done a deal together, even though we saw each other almost every Sunday at a great neighborhood restaurant in south Tulsa.

My first question was, "You used to do a lot of guaranteed lending, and I know you made a lot of money doing those loans. Why are you not doing them any more, with me or anyone else?"

He had a very surprising answer. He said, "Guaranteed lending just wasn't sexy enough!"

I wasn't sure I heard him correctly. He added that if people came to him as CEO of the bank and asked about applying for a loan and they were taken through a "guaranteed loan process," they would perceive that they were not considered the "best" client, because they needed a guarantee. "It's just not sexy enough!"

This was a huge revelation for me! No wonder banks are reluctant to get involved with these programs, I thought. And what a misperception and lost opportunity for the banks and their clients and communities.

As I mentioned at the outset, one of my goals is to share the truth about these programs with bankers like you because these programs are too valuable to overlook.

In this chapter, I share how most banks deal with guaranteed lending and offer specific suggestions for changing how these programs are positioned with bank management and boards, regulators, and customers.

Guaranteed lending is typically treated in one of four ways in a bank:

- It is completely ignored, because most banks don't know about it.

- In the unlikely instance that someone at the bank has heard about it, they don't touch it, because they believe it involves a long, complicated process, requiring more paperwork and specialized expertise than they can handle.

- When a bank does engage in guaranteed lending, it's mostly SBA, and is often delegated to the least experienced loan officer to "learn" the program and flounder around, working with doughnut shops, flower shops, franchises, etc.

- Sometimes a bank sets up a "guaranteed lending machine," where all guaranteed loans, typically SBA, are funneled and done. BancFirst in Oklahoma, headed by Kent Faison, has successfully done this and continues to be the largest and most successful SBA lender in the state.

We don't recommend the USDA guaranteed loan program as a high-volume program requiring a specialized department focused exclusively on this program. We recommend that a bank do no more than three or four of these loans per year. They should typically be larger deals representing a substantial gross volume, which have the potential to result in staggering income.

The following chart illustrates how three well-placed loans can net a bank more than $1.5 million. This might not be sexy to Bank of America, J.P. Morgan, Chase, Citigroup, or Wells Fargo, but for *any* bank that needs an extra million dollars or so of income, I think this is sexy as hell!

BREAKDOWN FOR TWO B&I LOANS FOR A TOTAL OF $7 MILLION AND ONE CF LOAN FOR $10 MILLION

	B&I	CF	TOTAL
Number of Loans	2	1	3
Loan Amount	$ 7,000,000	$10,000,000	$ 17,000,000
Guaranteed Percentage	80%	90%	
Guaranteed Amount in Dollars	$ 5,600,000	$ 9,000,000	$ 400,000
Assumed Origination Fee	1%	1%	
Origination Amount in Dollars	$ 70,000	$ 100,000	$ 170,000
Assumed Premium Percentage	10%	10%	
Premium in Dollars	$ 560,000	$ 900,000	$ 1,460,000
Total Bank Income	$ 630,000	$ 1,000,000	$ 1,630,000
Total Bank Exposure	$ 1,400,000	$ 1,000,000	$ 2,400,000

These numbers will appeal to any savvy CEO and board of directors, quickly changing the perception of these guaranteed loan programs. And remember, they don't even require any increase in overhead.

WHAT IF THE GOVERNMENT DOESN'T PAY OFF ON THE GUARANTEE?

It is rare for the USDA to deny a guarantee. The following chart prepared by the Comptroller of the Currency says it all.

B&I GUARANTEED LOAN PROGRAM PERFORMANCE	FY2008	FY2009	FY2010
Loans submitted for B&I Program	803	726	1263
Loans approved for B&I Program	588	506	1027
Loans where banks sought guarantees	50	45	90
Loans where guarantees where partially denied	0	3	2
Loans where guarantees were fully denied	1	0	1

Note 1: This information provided by the Comptroller of the Currency in June 2012 from the Community Affairs Department regarding community development.

Note 2: According to the USDA, of the five loss claims that were partially denied in FY2009 and 2010, three were denied for negligent servicing by the lender that caused an increase in the loss amount. One was denied because of lender misrepresentation. Another case was denied because of excessive accrued interest.

Note 3: Of the two loss claims denied in full during FY 2008 and 2010, one was because of fraud and misrepresentation by the lender, and the second was because the lender failed to maintain its lien position on the collateral.

WHAT HAPPENS IF THERE IS A DEFAULT?

In the event of a default and liquidation, the process and timeline under the USDA guaranteed loan programs are described in the next chart. Note that between default and liquidation, agency written authorization is required for cumulative protective advances over $5,000. While attorney fees are not considered a protective advance, the USDA does pay half of the liquidation appraisal.

TIMELINE FOR DEFAULT AND LIQUIDATION

30 days	Lender notifies USDA of default
60 days	Lender and borrower meet with the USDA to discuss options
90 days	Loan is determined eligible for liquidation
120 days (30)	Lender submits proposed method of liquidation in writing
150 days (30)	USDA informs lender if liquidation plan occurs and pays half the liquidation appraisal
180 days (90)	Lender files an estimated loss claim, if liquidation will exceed 90 days, and interest accrual stops
During Liquidation	Lender files bimonthly 1980-44 and quarterly progress reports
Liquidation Completed	All collateral is liquidated, and final loss is determined
30 days	Lender submits a final report of loss (USDA will not guarantee after 30 days)
60 days	USDA makes loss payment after review of the final loss report and accounting of the collateral

WON'T THE GOVERNMENT GET ITS MONEY FIRST ON THE GUARANTEE?

There is a common misconception that the government always gets its money first, and the bank gets whatever is left over. That is the furthest thing from the truth. In the event of liquidation, the bank always receives its equal claim, or *pari passu*, portion of the proceeds from the liquidation, as well as the cost of liquidation.

SECTION 2: REGULATORS AND LOAN POLICIES

The most effective way to change regulators' perceptions of these programs is through complete documentation.

Each guaranteeing agency has its own requirements for documenting and servicing guaranteed loans. In our experience, the initial packaging documentation is very complete and extremely well received by the regulators. We have found that when a bank first gets into the guaranteed lending arena, regulators are very interested in how those initial loans are packaged, documented, and serviced for a variety of reasons. The main reason is that the deals are typically larger (even after the bank has sold off the guarantees). Once the regulators see the guaranteed packages as routine, they may still pull those loans for review, because they are often the most organized and easiest-to-follow files in a bank's portfolio.

CHANGES IN LOAN POLICIES

We recommend that you change your bank's loan policies to include the use of guaranteed lending. This is fairly simple to do. I have convinced a couple of banks and their regulators to make this kind of policy change by showing the goals and uses for the guaranteed lending program. A typical board objection centers on the guaranteed programs' longer terms, which are contrary to most commercial lending bank policies. The longer term is typically the only real advantage to the borrower. (We'll discuss this more in the next section on customers' perceptions.) The government is giving the bank a 75 percent to 90 percent guarantee to go for the longer term. Remember that the bank is selling the guaranteed portion off into the secondary market, so you don't have all that capital tied up for the long term. In addition, the bank receives a much higher return on those amounts outstanding because of the servicing fees collected on the guaranteed portion of the loans. (See a discussion of the secondary market in Chapter 6.)

As for changing the bank's loan policy, all it takes is insertion of the following language: "... unless the loan carries a full faith and credit guarantee of the United States Government, at which point it will follow the rules and guidelines of the agency guaranteeing the loan." This phrase can be inserted in the sections on loan to value, terms, service area, interest rates, lending limits, and equity requirement.

IF IT NEEDS A GUARANTEE, ISN'T IT LIKELY TO BE A BAD LOAN?

How many times have you heard this from regulators? You can explain that you are using the guaranteed loan program just as the Comptroller of the Currency recommended in the June 2012 issue of Community Developments Insights. A copy of this publication can be found on the government site (www2.occ.gov) or you can find it directly at www.TheUSDALoanExperts.com/ComptrollerReportJune2012. Specifically the loans:

1. **Mitigate Risk**—You are not using the guarantee to make substandard loans but to mitigate the risk of financing buildings and equipment in rural America.

2. **Maximize Stockholder Returns**—You are maximizing stockholder returns by selling the guarantees for a premium and/or for servicing income.

3. **Manage Capital**—Selling off the guarantees minimizes the use of bank capital and at the same time maximizes the return on the outstanding capital, and it grows that capital base through increased net income.

SERVICING PROCEDURES

Servicing under the USDA guaranteed loan programs is very routine:

- Semi-annual financial statements (by the twentieth of the following month)
- Annual financial statements (reviewed by an outside CPA)
- Corporate tax return (required by the due date of the return or extension)
- Annual personal financial statement (due each January, signed and dated)
- Personal tax return (required by due date of the return or extension)
- Annual site visit and credit review

In addition to the typical servicing plan, there is a quarterly "online" report (see Form RD 1980-41 in Appendix C). This form is very simple to complete, especially since this is not a high-volume (number of loans) program.

Regulators are interested to discover that these loans are serviced as well as or better than the normal loans carried by the bank.

SECTION 3: CUSTOMERS

We believe that customer reservations regarding guaranteed loans are by far the easiest set of perceptions to change. Remember the banker who thought that guaranteed lending just wasn't sexy enough to offer a client? For bankers, like you, who want to provide true service to new or existing clients, here are six key advantages to emphasize regarding guaranteed loan programs:

1. **Longer Terms**—Conventional bank loans must be renewed every three to five years, involving cost, paperwork, and risk of loan denial. USDA guaranteed loans, on the other hand, offer longer terms, with no balloons or calls, and in the process they can also improve the borrower's cash flow. Consider the following guaranteed loan terms:

    a. **Land and building**—Up to thirty years for the B&I loan, while the CF program allows amortization up to forty years

    b. **Equipment**—Up to fifteen years, or the useful life of the equipment

    c. **Working capital**—Up to seven years (note that these programs do not work for lines of credit)

2. **Larger Loans Based on Loan to Value**—Customers can borrow more money under the USDA program with a new loan or a refinancing, because the loan-to-value (LTV) ratio is based on the appraised value, not book value or cost.

3. **More Lenient Equity Requirements**—The USDA equity requirements are much lower than normal banking requirements. The USDA utilizes a "post closing-tangible book equity calculation." For existing businesses, the requirement is only 10 percent, and for a start-up, it is 20 percent. The USDA is the only organization I know that has ever used these criteria.

4. **Assumable Loans**—The USDA guaranteed loan is assumable if approved by both the bank and the USDA. I have used this program as part of an exit strategy for borrowers who seek to sell their business in the next three to five years. The first step in the process is for the current successful owner to maximize his leverage on the existing assets for as long a term as possible. Then, in two to five years, when the owner is ready to sell, the prospective qualified buyers are able to come to the table with much less cash to purchase the company. Win-win! Doing business with USDA guaranteed loans may even lead to a higher asking price for the company since the assumable loan option makes it much easier for the buyer. In addition, the assumption does not trigger an event of prepayment, allowing the bank to build in a higher prepayment penalty, which results in higher premiums when sold into the secondary market.

5. **Flexible Interest Rates**—The bank and the client are free to negotiate interest rates, ranging from variable or fixed to five-year, ten-year, and fifteen-year adjustable (see Chapter 6 on the secondary market).

6. **Exclusive Loan Program**—Your bank is likely to make only a few of these loans per year. While they may take longer to put together, what makes them worth it is the

larger loan size for a longer term. We recommend that you emphasize to your customer that you have selected their project for one of the exclusive (two or three) guaranteed loan deals you will be doing in a given year. Make it unique and special, because it is!

ABOUT THE FEES

A bank seeking to lure a client away from a competitor bank across town may find that the client is really hung up on the fees. Under USDA programs, typical fees are 3 percent of the guarantee for a B&I loan and 1 percent of the guarantee for a CF loan. This is higher than a normal commercial loan, however, remember the term is considerably longer with no need for renewals and renewal fees every five to seven years with the possible risk of nonrenewal for any reason.

The bank is allowed to negotiate with the client an origination fee of up to 1 percent of the total loan. Your bank could find additional negotiating room by not charging or by reducing the origination fee substantially, including a high pre-payment penalty, or covering some or all of the fees, in anticipation of selling the loan for a substantial premium. Note: The sale of the guarantee can be negotiated long before the loan is sold. I will cover the secondary market in Chapter 6.

ARE THE FEES TOO HIGH?

Most clients will pay the fees once they understand that all of the fees and expenses can be financed into the deal. In addition, this is a one-time expense, compared to renewal fees every five to seven years with a traditional commercial loan, not to mention the risk of non-renewal at those times.

Chapter 4

YOUR BEST MARKETING OPPORTUNITIES AND HOW TO REACH THEM

LET'S SAY AT this point that you've sold your management team and your board on USDA guaranteed loans, and you've talked to your regulators and gotten their OK on this new approach. You may even have changed your loan policies as we suggested. Now how do you market the program?

In this chapter we suggest a highly effective strategy of hosting seminars and describe three promising target markets, two of which are really marketing partners: economic development and Chamber of Commerce officials and commercial Realtors. I'll also point you toward current and potential borrowers.

SEMINARS

Hosting seminars for clients and potential clients can position your bank as the leading bank authority on USDA guaranteed lending in your market. You can bring in leading authorities, like myself or any of our team, to conduct the seminars. As part of our coaching program, we provide our banks with PowerPoint presentations for these seminars, and they are available exclusively to your market.

Potential topics for seminars (based on the seminars we offer for our coaching clients):

- The Best Kept Secret to Financing Your Rural Business
- Long-Term Financing for Growth and Expansion
- Who Says There Is No Fixed-Rate Long-Term Money Available?
- Refinance Your Business as an Exit Strategy
- Health Care Financing

ECONOMIC DEVELOPMENT AND CHAMBER OF COMMERCE OFFICIALS

We have found it best first to identify those towns and cities in your market area that qualify for both the B&I program and CF program. Remember, the rules are different. The next step is to contact their various economic development organizations (local, regional, and statewide) and offer to provide specialized financing programs and educational seminars to their members and potential members.

You can offer to partner with them to assist existing businesses to grow, expand, acquire additional business, build a new building, or buy the building they are currently leasing. Or you can help them attract new businesses with unique financing to build a new facility or purchase that empty plant down the street.

We recognize the difficulty that rural communities with outdated health care facilities have in attracting new businesses. In the next chapter, we show how you can use the USDA guaranteed lending programs to facilitate the replacement or updating of a small or Critical Access Hospital (CAH) in a small town, which in turn can dramatically enhance the economic viability of the community by adding a large employer or improving the town's appeal.

COMMERCIAL REALTORS

The USDA B&I guaranteed lending program is a unique and ideal method of financing for commercial lending deals. If you know of commercial space for sale, we recommend that you contact the listing Realtor with an offer of assistance. Or perhaps you could team up with a Realtor around an empty manufacturing building in the community. As a leading authority on USDA guaranteed lending in your area, you can show economic developers how to attract and qualify a buyer with thirty-year terms, WABS (With Approved Balance Sheet) instead of WAC (With Approved Credit), and a variety of special interest rates. They might even decide to hand over the financing aspect of the deal to you.

A second approach involves educating commercial Realtors through sponsoring seminars that we could conduct for you. Be sure to take every opportunity to present to these folks, by inviting them to your bank, visiting their offices, or attending Realtor association gatherings. We have found that it takes a number of exposures to the programs before stakeholders really understand their true value.

CURRENT AND POTENTIAL BORROWERS

With USDA guaranteed loan programs, your bank now has something that other banks don't. First, you can offer your and other banks' customers an alternative to the three-to-five-year loan, with low risk. Second, for any business positioning itself for sale in the next few years, guaranteed loans are assumable, based on the bank's and USDA's approval. This is a definite advantage, requiring the buyer to come up with much less cash for the transaction, and could add real value to the business. Third, with the USDA program and the secondary market, you can offer many interest rate options.

As you can see in Appendix E, the guaranteed portion of the loans can be sold at par, to a variety of buyers, including Farmer Mac II, LLC. The Weekly Rate Line shows you a variety of options available to the bank. You will see there are fixed, floating, and adjustable rates at time periods including three-, five-, ten- and fifteen-year intervals. This will be discussed in more detail in Chapter 6, "The Secondary Market."

Chapter 5

UNIQUE LENDING OPPORTUNITIES THAT BENEFIT YOUR COMMUNITY

THE FIRST OBVIOUS new opportunity these guaranteed lending programs bring to smaller banks is an ability to do larger loans, because only the unguaranteed portion of the loan counts against the legal lending limit. You may be a small bank, but you can leverage yourself into a position of clout in your market. Another benefit to your bank in learning how to use these guaranteed loan programs is the resources you can bring to your community to assist in improving its infrastructure, specifically its health and welfare, cultural, and civic facilities.

One the very attractive options offered through the CF guaranteed lending program is the opportunity to finance hospital projects designed to make facilities conform with life/safety codes and Medicare and Medicaid requirements, as well as minor expansions needed to meet the immediate requirements of a community. As a community banker knowledgeable about this program, you can play a major role in upgrading your community's economic vitality by financing new or improved Critical Access Hospitals and other health care facilities in your area.

CRITICAL ACCESS HOSPITALS

As of September 30, 2012, there were 1,330 Certified Critical Access Hospitals (CAHs) located throughout the United States. Most of these were built during the 1950s and 1960s under the Hospital Survey and Construction Act (also known as the Hill-Burton Act) of 1946, which was designed to improve the facilities of the nation's hospital system. As of this writing, 60 percent to 70 percent of these hospitals need to be replaced or, at the very least, dramatically updated. We have seen a number of studies that assessed both alternatives and concluded that both options cost about the same. Why not build a new state-of-the-art facility?

An excellent marketing opportunity exists here. While you might run into resistance, such as the community thinking that it could not possibly afford to build a new hospital, we can show you how it can be done. Critical Access Hospitals can be reimbursed through Medicare for interest expense and depreciation for new or expanded facilities. This means that Medicare can pay for the new hospital.

We recommend that you directly approach all the CAHs in your state or specific service area. Through our affiliations and our exclusive Bank Coaching Program, we are able to arm you with a complete integrated turn-key process that includes master planning, right-sizing the new facility, feasibility, design, finance, engineering, construction, equipping, furnishing, and guidance through the Medicare inspection process. All this is included in a single, fixed-price contract that ensures your client that they will not be over budget due to contractor change orders. All this can be accomplished in half the time of normal construction.

You may save the hospital substantial funds by following our process. Sometimes such institutions jump forward, hiring an architect and starting the design process long before they confirm feasibility or financial ability. In fact, at a recent conference of the National Rural Health Association (NRHA), one hospital administrator and his team indicated that they had spent more than $1.5 million before they knew their project was either feasible or financeable. The integrated process we have developed reduces that cost substantially.

Even if a CAH has replaced its hospital in the last ten years or so, it could still be a candidate for any of the following:

- An expansion of the existing facility
- A new medical office building
- A dialysis center
- A new state-of-the-art emergency room and advanced telemedicine unit
- Advanced telemedicine units for an existing facility

Not only does the CF guaranteed loan program provide unique financing opportunities to the bank, but it also provides the bank with a very positive community exposure and good will for the project being financed, be it a new hospital, clinic, dialysis clinic, fire truck, or city hall.

Chapter 6

THE SECONDARY MARKET

MY FRIEND BRYAN tells the story of how in January 1991 he was being considered as a potential player for the Kansas City Royals in the Major League draft later that year. The problem was that, at the same time, Gulf War I was brewing in the Middle East. Bryan and his parents began to talk about what he'd do if he were drafted since he was only a junior in college and it would involve his leaving school early. Bryan's father, who was a World War II veteran, without hesitation, advised Bryan to join the Navy. Bryan and his mom laughed in amazement because while they were talking about the "draft" for baseball, his father had the military "draft" in his mind. The moral of the story is that, depending on our viewpoint and experience, the same term can mean different things.

In order to clarify the term "secondary market," let me explain exactly what it is from a big-picture view. The term purely relates to investors, banks, mutual funds, hedge funds, municipalities, or anyone who has the financial means to purchase a security offered by a broker who transacts the trade from one party to another. The stock market in a natural sense is a secondary market since, after a company sells its initial public offering (IPO), all other trades of that company's stock are between two parties unrelated to the company. For stocks, the NASDAQ Stock Market and the New York Stock Exchange (NYSE) are the places these stocks are traded and there is up-to-the second transparency of pricing. When it comes to bonds or U.S. government loan guarantees such as the ones produced through SBA or USDA financing, these items are placed for sale to brokerage firms who then offer a price for the security. Since there aren't billions of trades a day as we find in the stock market, the bond and loan guarantee secondary markets rely upon negotiations and competition between broker-dealers (brokerage firms). After a price is agreed upon, the brokerage firm will then purchase the security and resell it to another investor or one of its own clients with a mark-up (price increase). In this scenario, the bank will have sold the guarantee for a premium, the brokerage firm will have bought it and then sold it to one of its investors at an additional premium and the final investor will have bought a U.S. government-backed security that will yield a higher rate than a treasury bond or Ginnie Mae. It's truly a win-win-win for all parties. In fact, one of the largest buyers of USDA loan guarantees is Farmer Mac II, which is a government-sponsored entity whose mission it is to provide a secondary market for the guaranteed portions of USDA guaranteed loans.

LET'S JUMP INTO THE DETAILS

One of the most attractive aspects of USDA lending is the enhanced value available to lenders that sell the guaranteed portions of their loan originations into the secondary market. Because lenders retain the un-guaranteed portion of the loans on their books and continue to service the loans, valuable borrower relationships are not jeopardized. Selling the guaranteed portion into the secondary market allows lenders to originate loans that they might not otherwise make, due to legal lending limits, and, in some cases, to be competitive pricewise on loans that they might not otherwise be able to originate.

The secondary market also provides liquidity for additional lending and generates a substantial economic benefit to the institution. In fact, many lenders around the country have built their entire government guaranteed lending departments around secondary market sales and have turned those transactions into a profit center for their institutions.

The balance of this chapter will take a brief look at the key elements of secondary market sales, including the terms and conditions that affect the overall premium or servicing fees received and an overview of the process involved in secondary market sales. Our company, BF&D and The USDA Loan Experts, stands ready to assist your bank in maximizing its performance by selling the guaranteed portions of your loans into the secondary market.

The following three factors affect the overall premium or servicing fees received: the interest rate, the term, and prepayment penalties.

INTEREST RATES

The interest rate for the guaranteed loan is negotiated between the lender and the applicant and may be either fixed or variable, as long as it is a legal and customary rate. Interest rates are not allowed to be more than those rates customarily charged borrowers in similar circumstances in the ordinary course of business, and they are subject to agency review and approval. A variable interest rate agreed to by the lender and borrower must be a rate that is tied to a base rate agreed to by the lender and the agency. The variable interest rate may be adjusted at different intervals during the term of the loan, but the adjustments may not be made more often than quarterly and must be specified in the loan agreement. The normal base rate is Wall Street Journal Prime (WSJP). Obviously, higher variable interest rates will garner higher premiums. Unlike SBA terms, under the USDA guaranteed loan programs lenders do not have to split the premium that exceeds 10 percent with the SBA.

TERMS

Longer terms will also provide higher premiums, even though the average life, regardless of the term of a B&I loan, is approximately eight and a half years.

PREPAYMENT PENALTIES/LOCK-OUTS

The prepayment penalty is not restricted by the USDA and is negotiated between the borrower and the lender. The higher and longer the prepayment penalty, the higher the premium will be. Typical prepayment penalties are 5, 4, 3, 2, 1, or 8, 6, 4, 2, 1 or 5 percent for 5 years:

Year 1	5% Penalty	8% Penalty	5% Penalty
Year 2	4% Penalty	6% Penalty	5% Penalty
Year 3	3% Penalty	4% Penalty	5% Penalty
Year 4	2% Penalty	2% Penalty	5% Penalty
Year 5	1% Penalty	1% Penalty	5% Penalty

It is somewhat easier for the bank to negotiate these prepayment penalties in today's market for two key reasons. First, these loans are assumable, and, second, borrowers have fewer options today to borrow money. Needless to say, today's lending environment is truly a lender's market instead of what occurred a few years ago when it was a borrowers market and they could shop terms, rates and more. We don't see this changing for another three to five years.

EXAMPLE

Let's examine the economics of a secondary market sale. First, assume you have originated the following USDA guaranteed loan:

LOAN DESCRIPTION	
Loan Type:	USDA Guaranteed Loan
Borrower:	ABC Manufacturing LLC
Total Loan Amount:	$5,000,000
Guaranteed Percentage:	80%
Guaranteed Portion:	$4,000,000
Interest Rate Type:	Variable Rate
Variable Interest Rate Formula:	Prime Rate + 2.50%, Adjusted Quarterly
Interest Rate Caps/Floors:	No Caps or Floors
Payment Frequency:	Monthly P&I
Prepayment Penalties:	5-4-3-2-1%
Stated Maturity:	30 Years

To obtain a secondary market bid for the loan, lenders simply fill out and provide us with a standard bid request form (readily available) that essentially contains the information listed above. The bidder will specifically request any additional information or clarifications that may be required in order to formulate a bid. While it is not required, most lenders do retain a servicing fee on the sold portion of the loan. While the fee varies, it is the lender's choice. Most lenders keep 50-basis points of servicing.

For the purpose of our example, let's assume you have chosen to retain 50-basis points of servicing. We will further assume that the bidder has responded to you with a bid of $112.00. Now, let's examine the economic impact of the transaction. Please keep in mind that this example does not take into account the amortization of the loan or your internal accounting treatment of the transaction. It is simply intended to familiarize you with the basic economics of a secondary market transaction. To that end, here's an overview of the sale and a simple analysis of the transaction results:

SECONDARY MARKET SALE	
Amount Sold (*guaranteed portion*):	$4,000,000
Net Amt Invested After Sale (*un-gtd portion*):	$1,000,000
Borrower Rate:	Prime Rate+2.50% = 5.750% Current Rate
Lender Servicing:	50-basis points
Secondary Market Rate:	Prime Rate+2.000% = 5.250% Current Rate
Sale Price:	$112.000

SIMPLE RETURN ANALYSIS	
FIRST YEAR:	
Earn Premium on Sale [GTD PORTION X 12%]:	$ 480,000
Earn Full Rate on Retained Portion [UNGTD PORTION X 5.75%]:	$ 57,500
Earn Servicing on Sold Portion [GTD PORTION X 0.50%]:	$ 20,000
TOTAL FIRST YEAR'S EARNINGS:	$ 557,500
FIRST YEAR SIMPLE RETURN ON INVESTED DOLLARS [1ST YR EARNINGS/INVESTED AMT]:	55.75%
SUBSEQUENT YEARS:	
Earn Full Rate on Retained Portion [UNGTD PORTION X 5.75%]:	$ 57,500
Earn Servicing on Sold Portion [GTD PORTION X 0.50%]:	$ 20,000
SUBSEQUENT YEAR'S ANNUAL EARNINGS:	$ 77,500
SUBSEQUENT YEARS SIMPLE RETURN ON INVESTED DOLLARS [EARNINGS/INVESTED AMT]:	7.75%

As you can see, selling the guaranteed portion of the loan into the secondary market substantially enhances returns.

The following shows sample transactions where the loans are sold for a premium, servicing, or a combination of both.

	SELLING FOR PREMIUM	SELLING FOR SERVICING	50% PREMIUM 50% SERVICING
Loan Amount *Stated Rate at beginning*	$10,000,000 5.50%	$10,000,000 5.50%	$ 10,000,000 5.50%
Non-Guaranteed Portion	$ 2,000,000	$ 2,000,000	$ 2,000,000
Guaranteed Amount	$ 8,000,000	$ 8,000,000	$ 8,000,000
Premium at 10% Origination Fee 1%	$ 800,000 $ 100,000	$ 0 $ 100,000	$ 400,000 $ 100,000
Servicing Fee *(declines Annually)*	$ 0	$ 160,000	$ 80,000
Year One Yield on loan held	45.5%	18.5%	20.25%
Continuing Yield	5.5%	13.5%	12.25%

[1] Interest Rate – WSJP + 2.25%, no Floor or Ceiling, Adjusted Quarterly

Our typical recommendation to our bank coaching clients is generally to do a couple of USDA guaranteed loans, selling the guarantees for premium, and then to begin doing 50/50 premium/servicing. This is really determined by your board of directors and your need for short- term or long-term returns.

As noted previously, there is a very active secondary market for the USDA guaranteed loans but you must know how to deal with the brokerage firms and entities purchasing loan guarantees. Remember, they are looking to get the best possible deal for them. The key to attaining the best offer for the bank is negotiating with every firm from a position of strength and through competition. That is why we highly recommend that the bank get a number of quotes from the market to maximize the premium and/or spread on each loan.

MARKET UPDATE, EARLY 2013

A constant question asked by many bankers since 2008 has been whether the secondary market for USDA guaranteed loans dissolved during the banking collapse as the SBA markets did. The answer is NO. The premiums went as low as 5 percent, but they were always available. One of the main reasons for the difference between the USDA and SBA secondary market actions during the economic downturn are that SBA loans are often pooled and sold with many poolers. Since many of the poolers left the market for a few years, this temporarily eliminated the SBA secondary market.

The premiums in the USDA Secondary Market at the writing of this book were as high as 14.77, which is lower than the SBA market today by three hundred to four hundred basis points. However, don't forget that the lender does not have to share any part of the premium of the USDA loan guarantee sale, as in the case of SBA. The net effect can be seen as follows:

	USDA LOAN	SBA LOAN
Amount	$ 1,000,000.00	$ 1,000,000.00
Guarantee Percentage	80%	75%
Guarantee Amount	$ 800,000.00	$ 750,000.00
Premium Percentage	14%	18%
Premium in Dollars	$ 112,000.00	$ 135,000.00
Less: Amount Paid Agency	-	$ 30,000.00
Net Premium to Bank	$ 112,000.00	$ 105,000.00
Plus: Orignation Fee	$ 10,000.00	-
Total Net to Bank	$ 122,000.00	$ 105,000.00

Note: A special thanks to Joel Banes and Scott Taylor with Banes Capital, a leading buyer of SBA 7(a) and USDA Loans in Memphis, Tennessee, for their assistance with this chapter.

Chapter 7

THE COACHING PROGRAM

THIS BOOK HAS given an overview of how to use USDA guaranteed loan programs to boost your bank's bottom line while improving your community. Perhaps, however, you are interested in taking the information presented here to a deeper level, and would like an experienced partner for this process. I've mentioned our bank coaching program briefly throughout the book, but I wanted to take the opportunity to explain the process in more detail.

The comprehensive bank coaching program offered by The USDA Loan Experts, a division of Business Finance & Development (BF&D), introduces banks to the USDA's underutilized guaranteed loan programs, as does this book. We recognize, however, that bankers have to deal with an abundance of rules and regulations, and that choosing to begin working with these guaranteed lending program adds another level of paperwork. Through our coaching program, we aid bankers like you in practical ways, allowing your bank to leverage these programs to great advantage to you and to your community, with minimal risk and surprisingly high returns.

As our coaching client, your bank will be able to benefit from these advantages:

- Immediate access to product and industry knowledge
- Flexibility and speed to market with ideas and applications
- Increased lending opportunities in both size and type of loan, with less risk
- Increased lending liquidity, because only the nonguaranteed portion of the loan counts against the bank's legal lending limits
- Increased revenues and loan yields, without additional fixed costs
- Strong secondary market negotiating tactics
- No additional staffing requirements
- Access to our catalog of bank loan documents, with no additional software requirements

Our coaching program is unique, extending way beyond the typical "how-to" program. We support your staff for an entire year, walking through the programs and processes for your first loans. We will help your bank generate at least $20 million of guarantees during our coaching program. Our coaching program includes a guarantee that the bank will not lose money.

The program includes:

- In-depth education about the USDA's Business and Industry Program and Community Facilities Program

- A unique marketing strategy with specific targets within your service area

- Assistance aligning each project to fit into the USDA criteria, as well as ways to structure the deals to maximize premiums and/or service income

- Packaging tips that have been very well received in most of the USDA offices in the United States

- Navigation through the USDA process, to avoid common pitfalls and problems

- Secondary market strategies to maximize premiums and/or servicing income

- Servicing strategies

- Information about the liquidation process

- Case studies of successful loans

Our Coaching Program Guarantee: We will not offer our coaching services to another bank in your market or the geographical area we mutually agree upon. In addition, we guarantee profitability as long as the bank uses its best efforts.

Finally, we have only one rule in our company regarding clients we work with: If we don't like the individual or bank, we don't work with them. We had two deals go bad before we implemented this rule; had that rule been in place, we would not have entered into either deal. We will apply the same rule in selecting banks for our coaching program. I have discovered that life is way too short to deal with people you don't like.

That also means that if you don't like me, we won't work together. The best referral I ever received was from a client I fired because he and I didn't get along. He appreciated my honesty and still offered a reference to a colleague, encouraging him to talk with me because of my rule. That led to a great working relationship with the new client!

We realize that this program may not be for every bank. However, if your bank is ready to become a high-performing lending institution by increasing shareholder returns and non-interest income in ways your competition may not, please call our office at (918) 369-8516, extension 1, or contact us at greg@TheUSDALoanExperts.com to schedule a meeting.

Bonus 1

BASIC STEPS FOR PROCESSING A USDA B&I GUARANTEED LOAN

WHILE THE FOLLOWING outline lays out the basic steps in processing a USDA guaranteed loan, remember that some steps may vary from state to state.

1. **Determine Project Eligibility:**

    a. **Location**—Are the assets being financed located in a qualifying area? Here is the website that can be used to determine location eligibility:

    http://eligibility.sc.egov.usda.gov/eligibility/welcomeAction.do.

    It will take a couple of steps to get to the actual qualifier. Select "Business Programs" on the left hand column under "Property Eligibility." Then choose "Click here for the following programs," where you will find the Business and Industry

Guaranteed Loan Program. This will take you to the page where you will either "Accept" the property eligibility disclaimer or "Decline" it. You must accept it to move forward. You have finally reached the page where you can enter the address of the property, including a ZIP code. Then hit "Go," and the site should tell you whether the property qualifies.

b. **Collateral**—Is there adequate collateral to support the loan based upon the bank's loan policies and the USDA guidelines? At this point in the process, this is only an estimate. Remember, the values will be based on actual appraisals less than one year old. We recommend that money not be spent on new appraisals until the bank and the USDA approvals are obtained. As mentioned in Chapter 2, the following discounting is allowed:

Real Estate	80% of Appraised Value
Equipment	75% of Appraised Value
Accounts Receivable	75% to 80% of A/R less than 90 days current
Inventory	50% to 60% of cost

c. **Cash Flow**—Is there adequate cash flow to service the proposed debt? Ideally, historical cash flow will show 120 percent to 125 percent debt service coverage. Obviously, in the case of major expansions or start-up scenarios this cash flow will be based on projections. The bank must determine if the projections are reasonable. BF&D currently utilizes Sageworks software to analyze historical and projected cash flow by comparing it to industry averages. Anomalies can often be spotted and discussed with the client.

Cash flow is obviously one of the most important aspects of the loan analysis. The lender must be comfortable that there is adequate cash flow to service the proposed debt.

d. **Credit Worthy**—For me this is often very difficult because I do become invested in the projects and the people. Every lender has specific criteria to determine credit worthiness of clients. I would suggest that it's not always black and white. Some of our best clients have had some credit issues that had to be overcome. However, at the end of the day, the loans were approved and they continue to be great bank clients.

One example comes to mind is a client who had more than $350,000 of federal tax liens filed against the company, occurring in the middle of a major expansion. The company's bank immediately classified the loan and stopped the expansion.

The lien was caused by the embezzlement of funds by the company's bookkeeper. She had not paid payroll taxes and instead siphoned the funds to her account. She was arrested, prosecuted, and convicted and is now serving time in prison.

The company met with the IRS and began to pay $10,000 per month toward the amount total amount owed. While they had never missed a payment at the bank and were working with the IRS, there wasn't a bank in the area that would touch them due to the tax lien and classification. We were able to go to one of our bank coaching clients and got the deal done by refinancing their existing land, building, and equipment on a twenty-year term, allowed them to complete the construction of new offices and a showroom. They purchased new equipment, which expanded their capabilities, paying off the IRS after the agency forgave substantial penalties and interest. All this was done during the downturn in the economy. Today this company is profitable, with healthy cash flow, new facilities, expanded capabilities, and increased employment.

e. **Tangible Book Equity**—The USDA is the only organization I know that utilizes this kind of equity calculation. A minimum of 10 percent tangible balance sheet equity will be required for existing businesses at loan closing based on generally accepted accounting principals (GAAP). A minimum of 20 percent tangible balance sheet equity will be required for new businesses at loan closing. For energy projects, the minimum tangible balance sheet equity requirement range will be between 25 percent and 40 percent. What does this mean? This is a post-closing sample calculation as follows:

Total Assets	$2,500,000
Less: Intangible Assets[1]	$250,000
Tangible Assets	$2,250,000

---

[1] Intangible assets include loan closing costs, patents, copyrights, organization costs, goodwill, trade names, contracts, mailing lists, proprietary rights, brand names, and any items without tangible values.

Total Equity	$750,000
Less Intangible Assets	$250,000
	(same as above)
Tangible Equity	$500,000
Tangible Equity to Tangible Assets	$500,000/ $2,500,000 = 22.23%

Tangible Book Equity = Tangible Equity/ Tangible Assets

2. Structuring the Loan

This is probably where The USDA Loan Experts and BF&D add more value to the project than anywhere else in the process. Obviously this varies dramatically from deal to deal, but is often critical to the overall success of the project. Rarely is it as easy as simply presenting asset values and getting a quick answer as to how much the bank can lend.

A great example is where a client wants to refinance two assisted living centers for a total loan of $6 million. The bank, assuming the appraised value is $7.5 million, could lend the client $6 million, receiving a 70 percent guarantee. We would suggest that the borrower set up two separate LLCs or other company form. The bank can then lend $3 million to each LLC, both with an 80 percent guarantee. This is a perfectly acceptable structure under the USDA regulations:

> Option 1: A loan of $6 million with a $4.2 million (70 percent) guarantee

> Option 2: Two loans of $3 million each, totaling $6 million with $4.8 million (80 percent) guarantee

That's just one of many ways we can structure a loan to maximize the benefits for both the lender and borrower.

Our unique bank coaching program shows lenders a number of different tips and tricks to structure deals and even assist lenders all the way through $20 million of guarantees.

3. **Collection of Information**

    You've determined that the bank likes the project and has approved the loan "subject to appraisals and a guarantee from the USDA." Now it's time to collect the information necessary to complete the USDA application. We have provided a checklist of information that we use in gathering information for both the B&I and CF programs in Appendix F.

4. **Packaging**

    The "package" we refer to is actually the bank's application to the USDA requesting the guarantee. Unfortunately, states vary widely in what is required in the application and how it is presented. Check with your state office from its particular requirements. We have provided the table of contents we use in Appendix G. We have found this to be acceptable by most states for both the B&I and CF applications.

5. **Bank Loan Committee or Board Approval**

    It is necessary that the bank obtain all necessary approvals from either the loan committee or board of directors, depending on the bank's loan policy, prior to submitting the application to USDA. This will be included in the bank's credit memo, which must be included as part of the application. This memo requires some very specific items.

6. **Approved Bank Credit Memo**

   As mentioned above, the approved bank credit memo must be included in the application with all necessary signatures. Based on the USDA requirements the credit memo must include, along with lender's analysis, the following:

   1. Balance sheets and income statements for three years for established companies or a proforma balance sheet for a start-up

   2. Two years of projected year-end balance sheets and income statements with appropriate ratios and comparison with industrial standards (such as B&B, RMA)[2]

   3. Additional items:

      a. The borrower's management
      b. Repayment ability
      c. History of debt repayment
      d. Necessity for any debt refinancing, because terms are not favorable for the long term.
      e. Credit reports for the borrower, including the company's principals, and any parent, affiliate, or subsidiary firms.

---

[2] All data must be shown in total dollars and also in common size form, obtained by expressing all balance sheet items as a percentage of assets, and all income and expenses as a percentage of sales.

For coaching clients, BF&D provides financial analysis through our Sageworks software that meets some of the requirements above.

7. **Complete Necessary Appraisals and/or Feasibility, If Required**

   It's really up to the bank as to when the appraisals are obtained. If there are any questions as to collateral value, the appraisals should be ordered and included in the package. If the bank is comfortable that the values are there, then we suggest that the appraisals are not obtained till you have preliminary approval from the USDA, subject to the appraisals.

   The USDA may require a financial feasibility study if the project is a start-up or if there is a question as to overall viability. We were recently required to obtain a feasibility study on a new dialysis center proposed for a community in rural Oklahoma. The study indicated that there were more than ninety patients who were currently on dialysis within twenty-five miles of the proposed location. Break-even for the facility was fewer than twenty patients and 120 percent debt service coverage was reached at less than forty patients. The project was deemed feasible based on the study. USDA provides a guide for the financial feasibility, included in Appendix H.

8. **Application Signatures**

   Before submitting the completed application to USDA the borrower will need to sign Part A of Form RD 4279-1 of the application, as well as the Form RD 1940-20, Request For Environmental Information. The bank is also required to sign Part B of Form RD 4279-1 of the application.

9. **Submission of Package to USDA**

   As we have discussed, each state operates differently. In some states the application must be submitted to a regional office while in other states the application is submitted to the state office. Banks should contact the program director for the B&I Program and the CF programs to determine the state's preferred process.

   For our coaching clients we familiarize ourselves with all procedures for each state we work in prior to submission. Because of our experience and connections, we are sometimes able to obtain special permission to submit the packages directly to the state office, bypassing the regional offices and saving a substantial amount of time.

10. **Site Visit by USDA**

    USDA will typically do a site visit to the project. Again, depending on the state, USDA officials may want to meet the lending bank and the client at the same time. We have worked in some states where officials never do a comprehensive site visit but rather do a simple drive-by on their own, never meeting the client or the banker. We highly recommend that the bank try to control this process by actually scheduling the site visit in advance. We did have an unfortunate event one time where the USDA underwriter decided to make an unscheduled site visit. The project was the financing of an acquisition. When the USDA went to the site and announced what they were there for, the employees were surprised, as they knew nothing of the sale. You want to avoid that kind of situation.

11. USDA Underwriting

USDA typically has a loan specialist that will do the underwriting, not unlike the bank's underwriting process. This underwriting will include additional requirements to determine that all aspects of the USDA regulations, such as the rural location, equity requirements, and use of funds, are met.

12. USDA Committee Meeting for Approval

The state loan committee is often made up of four individuals, including the state director—a political appointee—the program director and one or two others selected by the state director. This committee has the final approval for the loans up to authorized limits. These limits vary state by state and between programs. If the loan request exceeds the authority of the state, the state committee will pass the final approval to Washington. Unfortunately, this can add additional time to the overall process. To speed this process, you should make sure you know the lending authority prior to the submission of the application.

13. USDA Conditional Commitment

Once the proper authorities have approved the loan, a conditional commitment will be issued to the bank (see ample in Appendix I). The bank must review this document carefully. This is the only approval document the bank will receive, and it is "conditional" subject to the bank's and client's meeting all the requirements listed on the commitment.

14. **Negotiate Conditional Commitment if required**

    This document is negotiable. Don't be afraid to discuss any point of this document with your USDA contact. We have often found that there are errors in the document that, if not corrected, could affect the bank and your client for the life of the loan. We have found that they often use the conditional commitment from the previous deal and all required changes had not occurred.

15. **Meet Conditions on Conditional Commitment**

    This is pretty self-explanatory, but please note that some of these conditions cannot be meet until closing actually occurs.

16. **Complete Loan Documents**

    One of the many advantages of USDA over the SBA is that the bank is allowed to use its own loan documents, except for a Form 4279-14 unconditional guarantee, which is signed by the borrower for everyone who owns 20% or more. Be certain that all items that need to be covered match the conditional commitment, especially including the loan covenants. We also recommend that once the loan documents are completed they be submitted to USDA prior to closing in order to eliminate any questions. This can really save time and assure the bank there are no issues that could delay the issuance of the guarantee. If the bank is selling the guaranteed portion of the note, the assignments should be completed and ready for USDA signatures and sent to the USDA at the same time as executed loan documents.

17. **Closing**

    The bank will close the loan in the usual manner, obtaining all necessary signatures, lien filings, and documentation. The borrower and the bank are required to sign off on the conditional commitment and return to USDA as part of the closing package.

18. **Closing Documents Plus Assignments Sent to USDA for Approval and Guarantee**

    All loan documents including the signed conditional commitment will be sent to USDA for review. Since they have already seen these documents, and provided no changes have occurred, this should be a relatively quick process. We have seen this process turned around the same day but have never seen it take more than five working days. This should be coordinated with the state office so that there are no delays in the process.

19. **USDA Signs and Returns Loan Note Guarantee and Signs Assignments to the Bank**

    USDA prepares and signs the loan note guarantee (see sample in Appendix J), along with the executed assignments to the bank, which is filed with the loan documents.

20. **Bank Funds the Loan**

    The bank has the guarantee, so they can fund the total amount of the loan without legal lending limit issues.

21. Bank Sends Assignments and Guarantee to a Secondary Market Buyer

Guarantees cannot be sold until the loan is fully funded if there happens to be a portion of the loan that is for construction. We recommend that, if a portion of the loan is for construction, the loan be broken into two separate notes where one note can be funded and sold while the construction portion is funded gradually until completion and inspection. When construction and inspection are complete, that portion of the loan will then be sold. All of this can be priced and determined prior to loan closing so that there will be no question as to the price the bank will receive for the premium.

22. Secondary Market Settlement

Once the secondary market buyer has good receipt, this buyer will fund the guaranteed amount plus the premium (if the loan is being sold for a premium) to the bank, typically within three business days.

23. Servicing

The proposed servicing plan is detailed in the application. This plan should be the bank's typical servicing requirements.

In addition, the USDA has a quarterly online reporting requirement that is very simple to complete. The agency will want to know the loan balance and whether the loan is current or delinquent (see Appendix D). The bank is also required to provide USDA with the minimum spread requirements and financial analysis standards required to comply with RD Instruction 4287-B, section 4287.107(d), and Form RD4279-4, "Lender's Agreement," paragraphs IV(c)(6) and (11). AN No. 4483 delineates the minimum financial analysis that the Business and Cooperative Programs believes a reasonably prudent lender would use for a performing loan. See Appendix K for a complete copy of AN 4483.

Remember, that this process is a low-volume, high-return program. We recommend to our coaching clients that the bank do two or three of these loans per year with little or no increase in overhead. As we discussed in Chapter 7, The USDA Loan Experts and BF&D has a bank coaching program that can get the bank up to speed on these programs quickly and efficiently with no additional staffing requirements.

Bonus 2

BANK BOARD PRESENTATION

Please go to our website at

www.TheUSDALoanExperts.com

to download our PowerPoint presentation for your bank's board of directors, and view a short video about the presentation.

Appendix A

USDA BUSINESS AND INDUSTRY GUARANTEED LOAN PROGRAM

Below are key excerpts from the USDA Community Facilities Guaranteed Loan Program instructions that we think you will find helpful. They address the most commonly asked questions. Complete instructions can be found at:

- RD 4279-A: http://www.rurdev.usda.gov/SupportDocuments/4279a.doc

- RD 4279-B: http://www.rurdev.usda.gov/SupportDocuments/4279b.doc

The USDA also publishes administrative notices intended to clarify or better interpret the regulations. While some of the administrative notices are published on the USDA website and sent to the state offices, not all are regularly published or distributed to participating banks. When you are a client in our coaching program, we will send new notices to you as soon as they are issued.

B&I EXCERPT 1

§ 4279.29 Eligible Lenders

(a) Traditional lenders. An eligible lender is any federal or state chartered bank, farm credit bank, other farm credit system institution with direct lending authority, bank for cooperatives, savings and loan association, or mortgage company that is part of a bank-holding company. These entities must be subject to credit examination and supervision by either an agency of the United States or a state. Eligible lenders may also include credit unions, provided they are subject to credit examination and supervision by either the National Credit Union Administration or a state agency, and insurance companies, provided they are regulated by a state or national insurance regulatory agency. Eligible lenders include the National Rural Utilities Cooperative Finance Corporation.

(b) Other lenders. Rural utilities service borrowers and other lenders not meeting the criteria of paragraph (a) of this section may be considered by the agency for eligibility to become a guaranteed lender, provided the agency determines that they have the legal authority to operate a lending program and sufficient lending expertise and financial strength to operate a successful lending program.

(1) Such a lender must:

(i) Have a record of successfully making at least three commercial loans annually for at least the most recent three years, with delinquent loans not exceeding 10 percent of loans outstanding and historic losses not exceeding 10 percent of dollars loaned, or when the proposed lender can demonstrate that it has personnel with equivalent previous experience and where the commercial loan portfolio was of a similar quantity and quality; and

(ii) Have tangible balance sheet equity of at least 7 percent of tangible assets and sufficient funds available to disburse the guaranteed loans it proposes to approve within the first six months of being approved as a guaranteed lender.

(2) A lender not eligible under paragraph (a) of this section that wishes consideration to become a guaranteed lender must submit a request in writing to the state office for the state where the lender's lending and servicing activity takes place. The state office will review the request and forward the request, with the state director's recommendations, to the national office for consideration. The national office will make such investigations as it deems necessary and will notify the prospective lender, through the state director, whether the lender's request for eligibility is approved or rejected. If rejected, the reasons for the rejection will be indicated to the prospective lender in writing. The lender's written request must include:

(i) Evidence showing that the lender has the necessary capital and resources to successfully meet its responsibilities.

(ii) Copy of any license, charter, or other evidence of authority to engage in the proposed loan making and servicing activities. If licensing by the state is not required, an attorney's opinion to this effect must be submitted.

(iii) Information on lending experience, including length of time in the lending business; range and volume of lending and servicing activity; status of loan portfolio, including delinquency rate, loss rate as a percentage of loan amounts, and other measures of success; experience of management and loan officers; audited financial statements not more than one year old; sources of funds for the proposed loans; office location and proposed lending area; and proposed rates and fees, including loan origination, loan preparation, and servicing fees. Such fees must not be greater than those charged by similarly located commercial lenders in the ordinary course of business.

(iv) An estimate of the number and size of guaranteed loan applications the lender will develop.

(c) Expertise. Loan guarantees will only be approved for lenders with adequate experience and expertise to make, secure, service, and collect B&I loans.

B&I EXCERPT 2

§ 4279.72 Conditions of Guarantee

A loan guarantee under this part will be evidenced by a loan note guarantee issued by the agency. Each lender will execute a lender's agreement. If a valid lender's agreement already exists, it is not necessary to execute a new lender's agreement with each loan guarantee. Original lender's agreements should be maintained in an operational file in a fire-resistant cabinet. Each case file should contain a copy of the applicable lender's agreement. The provisions of this part and part 4287 will apply to all outstanding guarantees. In the event of a conflict between the guarantee documents and these regulations as they exist at the time the documents are executed, the regulations will control.

(a) Full faith and credit. A guarantee under this part constitutes an obligation supported by the full faith and credit of the United States and is incontestable except for fraud or misrepresentation of which a lender or holder has actual knowledge at the time it becomes such lender or holder or which a lender or holder participates in or condones. The guarantee will be unenforceable to the extent that any loss is occasioned by a provision for interest on interest. In addition, the guarantee will be unenforceable by the lender to the extent any loss is occasioned by the violation of usury laws, negligent servicing, or failure to obtain the required security regardless of the time at which the agency acquires knowledge thereof. Any losses occasioned will be unenforceable to the extent that loan funds are used for purposes other than those specifically approved by the agency in its conditional commitment. The agency will guarantee payment as follows:

(1) To any holder, 100 percent of any loss sustained by the holder on the guaranteed portion of the loan and on interest due on such portion.

(2) To the lender, the lesser of:

(i) Any loss sustained by the lender on the guaranteed portion, including principal and interest evidenced by the notes or assumption agreements and secured advances for protection and preservation of collateral made with the agency's authorization

(ii) The guaranteed principal advanced to or assumed by the borrower and any interest due thereon

B&I EXCERPT 3

§ 4279.75 Sale or Assignment of Guaranteed Loan

The lender may sell all or part of the guaranteed portion of the loan on the secondary market or retain the entire loan. The lender shall not sell or participate any amount of the guaranteed or unguaranteed portion of the loan to the borrower or members of the borrower's immediate families, officers, directors, stockholders, other owners, or a parent, subsidiary, or affiliate company.

If the lender desires to market all or part of the guaranteed portion of the loan at or subsequent to the loan closing, such loan must not be in default. Loans made with the proceeds of any obligation the interest on which is excludable from income under 26 U.S.C. § 103 (interest on state and local banks) or any successor section will not be guaranteed. Options for sale and structure of the loan are outlined in Appendix B of Subpart B of this section.

(a) Single note system. The entire loan is evidenced by one note, and one loan note guarantee is issued. The lender may assign all or part of the guaranteed portion of the loan to one or more holders by using the agency's assignment guarantee agreement. The holder, upon written notice to the lender and the agency, may reassign the unpaid guaranteed portion of the loan sold under the assignment guarantee agreement. Upon notification and completion of the assignment through the use of Form 4279-6, the assignee shall succeed to all rights and obligations of the holder there under. If this option is selected, the lender may not at a later date cause any additional notes to be issued.

(b) Multi-note system. Under this option the lender may provide one note for the unguaranteed portion of the loan and no more than ten notes for the guaranteed portion. When this option is selected by the lender, the holder will receive one of the borrower's executed notes and a loan note guarantee. The agency will issue a loan note guarantee for each note, including the unguaranteed note, to be attached to the note. An assignment guarantee agreement will not be used when the multi-note option is utilized.

(c) After loan closing. If a loan is closed using the multi-note option and at a later date additional notes are desired, the lender may cause a series of new notes, so that the total number of notes issued does not exceed the total number provided for in paragraph (b) of this section, to be issued as replacement for previously issued guaranteed notes, provided:

(1) Written approval of the agency is obtained. The agency will issue the appropriate loan note guarantees to be attached to each of the new notes in exchange for the original loan note guarantee which will be canceled by the agency.

(2) The borrower agrees and executes the new notes.

(3) The interest rate does not exceed the interest rate in effect when the loan was closed.

(4) The maturity date of the loan is not changed.

(5) The agency will not bear or guarantee any expenses that may be incurred in reference to such reissuances of notes.

(6) There is adequate collateral securing the notes.

(7) No intervening liens have arisen or have been perfected and the secured lien priority remains the same.

(8) All holders agree.

B&I EXCERPT 4

§ 4279.76 Participation

The lender may obtain participation in the loan under its normal operating procedures; however, the lender must retain title to the notes if any of them are unguaranteed and retain the lender's interest in the collateral.

B&I EXCERPT 5

§ 4279.77 Minimum retention

The lender is required to hold in its own portfolio a minimum of 5 percent of the total loan amount. The amount required to be maintained must be of the unguaranteed portion of the loan and cannot be participated to another. The lender may sell the remaining amount of the unguaranteed portion of the loan only through participation.

B&I EXCERPT 6

4279.107 Guarantee fees (Revised 10-03-05, SPECIAL PN.)

For all new loans there are two types of nonrefundable guarantee fees to be paid by the lender. The fees may be passed on to the borrower. The fees may be forwarded to the agency through an electronic funds transfer system or, at the agency's discretion, by a check payable to USDA using a USDA-approved form.

(a) Initial guarantee fee. The initial fee is paid at the time the loan note guarantee is issued. The fee may be included as an eligible loan purpose in the guaranteed loan. The fee will be the rate (a specified percentage not to exceed 2 percent) multiplied by the principal loan amount, multiplied by the percent of guarantee. Subject to specified annual limits set by the Agency, the initial guarantee fee may be reduced to 1 percent if the borrower's business supports value-added agriculture and results in farmers benefiting financially, or

(1) is a high impact business development investment in accordance with § 4279.155(b)(5), and

(2) is located in a rural community that:

(i) is experiencing long-term population decline and job deterioration, or

(ii) has remained persistently poor over the last 60 years, or

(iii) is experiencing trauma as a result of natural disaster, or

(iv) is experiencing fundamental structural changes in its economic base.

(3) Written requests for approval of a guaranteed loan with the reduced guarantee fee must be forwarded to the national office, Attn: Director, Business Programs Processing Division, for review and consideration prior to obligation of the guaranteed loan. The administrator will provide a written response to the state director concerning the request confirming approval or disapproval of the request to approve the guaranteed loan with the reduced guarantee fee. After the guaranteed authority has been exhausted, the national office will provide guidance to the state directors.

(b) Annual renewal fee. The annual renewal fee is paid once a year and is required to maintain the enforceability of the guarantee as to the lender.

(1) The rate of the annual renewal fee (a specified percentage) is established by Rural Development in an annual notice published in the Federal Register, multiplied by the outstanding principal loan balance as of December 31 of each year, multiplied by the percent of guarantee. The rate is the rate in effect at the time the loan is obligated, and will remain in effect for the life of the loan.

(2) Annual renewal fees are due on January 31. Payments not received by April 1 are considered delinquent and, at the agency's discretion, may result in cancellation of the guarantee to the lender. Holders' rights will continue in effect as specified inthe loan note guarantee and assignment guarantee agreement. Any delinquent annual renewal fees will bear interest at the note rate and will be deducted from any loss payment due the lender. For loans where the loan note guarantee is issued between October 1 and December 31, the first

annual renewal fee payment will be due January 31 of the second year following the date the loan note guarantee was issued.

(a) Type of entity. A borrower may be a cooperative organization, corporation, partnership, or other legal entity organized and operated on a profit or nonprofit basis; an Indian tribe on a federal or state reservation or other federally recognized tribal group; a public body; or an individual. A cooperative organization is a cooperative or an entity, not chartered as a cooperative, that operates as a cooperative in that it is owned and operated for the benefit of its members, including the manner in which it distributes its dividends and assets. A borrower must be engaged in or proposing to engage in a business. Business may include manufacturing, wholesaling, retailing, providing services, or other activities that will: (Revised 12-22-04, PN 381.)

(1) Provide employment;

(2) Improve the economic or environmental climate;

(3) Promote the conservation, development, and use of water for aquaculture; or

(4) Reduce reliance on nonrenewable energy resources by encouraging the development and construction of solar energy systems and other renewable energy systems (including wind energy systems, geothermal energy systems, and anaerobic digesters for the purpose of energy generation). (Revised 12-22-04, PN 381.)

(b) Citizenship. Individual borrowers must be citizens of the United States (U.S.) or reside in the U.S. after being legally admitted for permanent residence. Citizens and residents of the Republic of Palau, the Federated States of Micronesia, and the Republic of the Marshall Islands shall be considered U.S. citizens. Corporations or other nonpublic body organization-type borrowers must be at least 51 percent owned by persons who are either citizens of the U.S. or reside in the U.S. after being legally admitted for permanent residence.

(c) Rural area. The business financed with a B&I Guaranteed Loan must be located in a rural area, except for cooperative organizations financed in accordance with paragraph (d)(3) of this section. Loans to borrowers with facilities located in both rural and non-rural areas will be limited to the amount necessary to finance the facility located in the eligible rural area, except for cooperative organizations financed in accordance with paragraph (d)(3) of this section. Rural areas are any areas other than: (Revised 12-22-04, PN 381.)

(1) A city or town that has a population of greater than 50,000 inhabitants; and

(2) The urbanized area contiguous and adjacent to such a city or town, as defined by the U.S. Bureau of the Census using the latest decennial census of the United States.

(3) Individuals that reside in the U.S. after being legally admitted for permanent residence must provide a permanent green card as evidence of eligibility. Temporary or conditional green cards or any type of visa, regardless of whether they may ultimately lead to acquiring a permanent green card, do not meet this requirement, e.g., E-2 or E-5 immigrant visas. (Added 10-26-11, PN 452.)

(4) Applications may not be approved subject to meeting citizenship requirements. (Added 10-26-11, PN 452.)

(d) Loans to cooperative organizations. (Added 12-22-04, PN 381.)

(1) B&I loans to eligible cooperative organizations may be made in principal amounts up to $40 million if the project is located in a rural area, the cooperative facility being financed provides for the value-added processing of agricultural commodities, and the total amount of loans exceeding $25 million does not exceed 10 percent of the funds available for the fiscal year.

(2) Cooperative organizations that are headquartered in a non-rural area may be eligible for a B&I loan if the loan is used for a project or venture that is located in a rural area.

(3) B&I loans to eligible cooperative organizations may also be made in non-rural areas provided:

(i) The primary purpose of the loan is for a facility to provide value-added processing for agricultural producers that are located within 80 miles of the facility;

(ii) The applicant satisfactorily demonstrates that the primary benefit of the loan will be to provide employment for rural residents;

(iii) The principal amount of the loan does not exceed $25 million; and

(iv) The total amount of loans guaranteed under this section does not exceed 10 percent of the funds available for the fiscal year.

(4) An eligible cooperative organization may refinance an existing B&I loan provided that the existing loan is current and performing, the existing loan is not and has not been in

payment default (more than 30 days late) or the collateral of which has not been converted, and there is adequate security or full collateral for the new B&I loan.

(e) Other Credit. All applications for assistance will be accepted and processed without regard to the availability of credit from any other source. Applicants are to be advised of other potential sources of credit but are not encouraged or required to pursue financing from any of these sources in lieu of assistance from the agency. (Renumbered 12-22-04, PN 381)

B&I EXCERPT 6

§ 4279.113 Eligible loan purposes

Loan purposes must be consistent with the general purpose contained in **§ 4279.101 of this subpart. They include but are not limited to the** following:

(a) Business and industrial acquisitions when the loan will keep the business from closing, prevent the loss of employment opportunities, or provide expanded job opportunities.

(b) Business conversion, enlargement, repair, modernization, or development.

(c) Purchase and development of land, easements, rights-of-way, buildings, or facilities.

(d) Purchase of equipment, leasehold improvements, machinery, supplies, or inventory.

(e) Pollution control and abatement.

(f) Transportation services incidental to industrial development.

(g) Startup costs and working capital.

(h) Agricultural production, when not eligible for Farm Service Agency (FSA) farmer program assistance and when it is part of an integrated business also involved in the processing of agricultural products.

> (1) Examples of potentially eligible production include but are not limited to: an apple orchard in conjunction with a food processing plant; poultry buildings linked to a meat processing operation; or sugar beet production coupled with storage and processing. Any agricultural production considered for B&I financing must be owned, operated, and maintained by the business receiving the loan for which a guarantee is provided. Independent agricultural production operations, even if not eligible for FSA farmer programs assistance, are not eligible for the B&I program.
>
> (2) The agricultural-production portion of any loan will not exceed 50 percent of the total loan or $1 million, whichever is less.

(i) Purchase of membership, stocks, bonds, or debentures necessary to obtain a loan from Farm Credit System institutions and other lenders provided that the purchase is required for all of their borrowers. (Revised 12-22-04, PN 381)

(j) Purchase of cooperative stock by individual farmers or ranchers in a farmer or rancher cooperative established for the purpose of processing an agricultural commodity. (Added 12-22-04, PN 381)

> (1) The cooperative may contract for services to process agricultural commodities or otherwise process value-added agricultural products during the 5-year period beginning on the

operation startup date of the cooperative in order to provide adequate time for the planning and construction of the processing facility of the cooperative.

(2) Notwithstanding §§ 4279.131(d) and 4279.137, the individual farmer or rancher may provide financial information in the manner that is generally required by commercial agricultural lenders in order to obtain a loan.

(k) Aquaculture, including conservation, development, and utilization of water for aquaculture. (Renumbered 12-22-04, PN 381)

(l) Commercial fishing. (Renumbered 12-22-04, PN 381)

(m) Commercial nurseries engaged in the production of ornamental plants and trees and other nursery products such as bulbs, flowers, shrubbery, flower and vegetable seeds, sod, and the growing of plants from seed to the transplant stage. (Renumbered 12-22-04, PN 381)

(n) Forestry, which includes businesses primarily engaged in the operation of timber tracts, tree farms, and forest nurseries and related activities such as reforestation. (Renumbered 12-22-04, PN 381)

(o) The growing of mushrooms or hydroponics. (Renumbered 12-22-04, PN 381.)

(p) Interest (including interest on interim financing) during the period before the first principal payment becomes due or when the facility becomes income producing, whichever is earlier. (Renumbered 12-22-04, PN 381)

(q) Feasibility studies. (Renumbered 12-22-04, PN 381)

(r) To refinance outstanding debt when it is determined that the project is viable and refinancing is necessary to improve cash flow and create new or save existing jobs. Except as provided for in § 4279.108(d)(4) of this subpart, existing lender debt may be included provided that, at the time of application, the loan has been current for at least the past twelve months (unless such status is achieved by the lender forgiving the borrower's debt) and the lender is providing better rates or terms. Subordinated owner debt is not eligible under this paragraph. Unless the amount to be refinanced is owed directly to the federal government or is federally guaranteed, the existing lender debt refinancing must be a secondary part (less than 50 percent) of the overall loan. (Revised 03-21-07, PN 407)

(s) Takeout of interim financing. Guaranteeing a loan after project completion to pay off a lender's interim loan will not be treated as debt refinancing provided that the lender submits a complete pre-application or application which proposes such interim financing prior to completing the interim loan. A lender that is considering an interim loan should be advised that the agency assumes no responsibility or obligation for interim loans advanced prior to the conditional commitment being issued. (Renumbered 12-22-04, PN 381)

(t) Fees and charges for professional services and routine lender fees. (Renumbered 12-22-04, PN 381)

(u) Agency guarantee fee. (Renumbered 12-22-04, PN 381)

(v) Tourist and recreation facilities, including hotels, motels, and bed and breakfast establishments, except as prohibited under ineligible purposes. (Renumbered 12-22-04, PN 381)

(1) Tourism and recreation projects can be a vital part of a rural area's economic development strategy. On the other

hand, they are typically difficult credit decisions due to the risks involved. You may want to obtain an independent feasibility study to make sure that demand, utilization, and related cash flow issues are looked at closely.

(2) Projects that are commonly not successful in the area normally should not be financed. This does not mean that new ventures should not be considered. It means, as a hypothetical example, that if five out of ten ski areas without snowmaking capabilities in Vermont have failed, such a recreational proposal probably carries excessive risk. Similar examples might be hotels or motels in many rural areas, outdoor tennis or swimming pools, or water slides in northern climates.

(3) Work closely with the lender, early in the process, on credit quality. Many requests will meet the "loan purpose" eligibility test but may not be credit worthy due to high risk.

(w) Educational or training facilities. (Renumbered 12-22-04, PN 381)

(x) Community facility projects which are not listed as an ineligible loan purpose such as convention centers. (Renumbered 12-22-04, PN 381)

(y) Constructing or equipping facilities for lease to private businesses engaged in commercial or industrial operations. (Renumbered 12-22-04, PN 381)

(z) The financing of housing development sites provided that the community demonstrates a need for additional housing to prevent a loss of jobs in the area or to house families moving to the area as a result of new employment opportunities. (Renumbered 12-22-04, PN 381) (aa) Community antenna television services or facilities. (Renumbered 12-22-04, PN 381)

(bb) Provide loan guarantees to assist industries adjusting to terminated Federal agricultural programs or increased foreign competition. (Renumbered 12-22-04, PN 381)

(cc) To finance energy projects. Commercially available energy projects that produce biomass fuel or biogas as an output must have completed two operating cycles at design performance levels submitted to the agency. Projects that produce steam or electricity as an output must have met or exceeded acceptance test performance criteria submitted to the agency and be successfully interconnected with the purchaser of the output. Performance or acceptance test requirements for all other energy projects will be determined by the agency on a case-by-case basis. Financing for energy projects will only be allowed when the facility has been constructed according to plans and specifications and is producing at the quality and quantity projected in the application. (Added 07-26-06, PN 400)

B&I EXCERPT 7

§ 4279.114 Ineligible purposes

(a) Distribution or payment to an individual owner, partner, stockholder, or beneficiary of the borrower or a close relative of such an individual when such individual will retain any portion of the ownership of the borrower

(b) Projects in excess of $1 million that would likely result in the transfer of jobs from one area to another and increase direct employment by more than fifty employees

(c) Projects in excess of $1 million that would increase direct employment by more than fifty employees, if the project would result in an increase in the production of goods for which there is not sufficient demand, or if the availability of services or facilities is insufficient to meet the needs of the business

(d) Charitable institutions, churches, or church-controlled or fraternal organizations

(e) Lending and investment institutions and insurance companies

(f) Assistance to Government employees and military personnel who are directors or officers or have a major ownership of 20 percent or more in the business

(g) Racetracks for the conduct of races by professional drivers, jockeys, etc., where individual prizes are awarded in the amount of $500 or more

(h) Any business that derives more than 10 percent of annual gross revenue from gambling activity

(i) Any illegal business activity

(j) Prostitution

(k) Any line of credit

(l) The guarantee of lease payments

(m) The guarantee of loans made by other federal agencies

(n) Owner-occupied housing. Bed and breakfasts, storage facilities, et al, are allowed when the pro rata value of the owner's living quarters is deleted.

(o) Projects that are eligible for the Rural Rental Housing and Rural Cooperative Housing loans under sections 515, 521, and 538 of the Housing Act of 1949, as amended

(p) Loans made with the proceeds of any obligation the interest on which is excludable from income under 26 U.S.C. § 103 or a successor statute. Funds generated through the issuance of tax-exempt obligations may neither be used to purchase the guaranteed portion of any agency guaranteed loan nor may an agency guaranteed loan serve as collateral for a tax-exempt issue. The agency may guarantee a loan for a project, which involves tax-exempt financing only when the guaranteed loan funds are used to finance a part of the project that is separate and distinct from the part, which is financed by the tax-exempt obligation, and the guaranteed loan has at least a parity security position with the tax-exempt obligation.

(q) The guarantee of loans where there may be, directly or indirectly, a conflict of interest or an appearance of a conflict of interest involving any action by the agency. An example of a conflict of interest would be where guaranteed funds are used to finance a federal office building where one of the tenants leasing the space is a USDA agency or organization.

(r) Golf courses

B&I EXCERPT 8

§ 4279.120 Fees and charges

(a) Routine lender fees. The lender may establish charges and fees for the loan provided they are similar to those normally charged other applicants for the same type of loan in the ordinary course of business.

(b) Professional services. Professional services are those rendered by entities generally licensed or certified by States or accreditation associations, such as architects, engineers, packagers, accountants, attorneys, or appraisers. The borrower may pay fees for professional services needed for planning and developing a project provided that the amounts are reasonable and customary in the area. Professional fees may be included as an eligible use of loan proceeds.

(c) Fee Review. You should review fees in the application but rely on the opinion of the lender as to their reasonableness.

B&I EXCERPT 9

§ 4279.125 Interest rates

The interest rate for the guaranteed loan will be negotiated between the lender and the applicant and may be either fixed or variable as long as it is a legal rate. Interest rates will not be more than those rates customarily charged borrowers in similar circumstances in the ordinary course of business and are subject to agency review and approval. Lenders are encouraged to utilize the secondary market and pass interest-rate savings on to the borrower.

(a) A variable interest rate agreed to by the lender and borrower must be a rate that is tied to a base rate agreed to by the lender and the agency. The variable interest rate may be adjusted at different intervals during the term of the loan, but the adjustments may not be more often than quarterly and must be specified in the loan agreement. The lender must incorporate, within the variable rate promissory note at loan closing, the provision for adjustment of payment installments coincident with an interest-rate adjustment. The lender will ensure that the outstanding principal balance is properly amortized within the prescribed loan maturity to eliminate the possibility of a balloon payment at the end of the loan.

(b) Any change in the interest rate between the date of issuance of the conditional commitment and before the issuance of the Loan Note Guarantee must be approved in writing by the agency approval official. Approval of such a change will be shown as an amendment to the conditional commitment.

(c) It is permissible to have one interest rate on the guaranteed portion of the loan and another rate on the unguaranteed portion of the loan provided that the rate on the guaranteed portion does not exceed the rate on the unguaranteed portion.

(d) A combination of fixed and variable rates will be allowed.

(e) While the lender and applicant negotiate the interest rate on a B&I loan, you have a responsibility as an agency loan officer to make sure that the rate is no more than that rate customarily charged borrowers under similar circumstances when there is no guarantee. You should encourage lenders, by counseling and the use of the priority ranking system, to pass the savings of the secondary market on to the borrower. Make sure that new lenders understand the requirements of this section early in the loan process.

B&I EXCERPT 10

§ 4279.126 Loan terms

(a) The maximum repayment for loans on real estate will not exceed 30 years; machinery and equipment repayment will not exceed the useful life of the machinery and equipment purchased with loan funds or fifteen years, whichever is less; and working capital repayment will not exceed seven years. The term for a loan that is being refinanced may be based on the collateral the lender will take to secure the loan. See Appendix B of this subpart for structuring multiple note loans.

(b) The first installment of principal and interest will, if possible, be scheduled for payment after the project is operational and has begun to generate income. However, the first full installment must be due and payable within three years from the date of the promissory note and be paid at least annually thereafter. Interest-only payments will be paid at least annually from the date of the note. Monthly payments will normally be expected except for seasonal-type businesses.

(c) Only loans that require a periodic payment schedule, which will retire the debt over the term of the loan without a balloon payment, will be guaranteed.

(d) A loan's maturity will take into consideration the use of proceeds, the useful life of assets being financed, and the borrower's ability to repay the loan. The lender may apply the maximum guidelines specified above only when the loan cannot be repaid over a shorter term.

(e) All loans guaranteed through the B&I program must be sound, with reasonably assured repayment.

B&I EXCERPT 11

§ 4279.131 Credit quality

The lender is primarily responsible for determining credit quality and must address all of the elements of credit quality in a written credit analysis including adequacy of equity, cash flow, collateral, history, management, and the current status of the industry for which credit is to be extended. In reviewing the lender's analysis and related materials, pay particular attention to working capital since it is usually critical to project success.

(a) Cash flow. All efforts will be made to structure or restructure debt so that the business has adequate debt coverage and the ability to accommodate expansion. The ability to repay a loan from the cash flow of the business is the most important consideration in the loan making process. You should not approve loan guarantee requests that do not show repayment ability. Historical operation reports are the best basis to evaluate cash flow. Review interim operating statements carefully, for they are just that, interim statements. Use a realistic projection of future earnings. Test such a projection against industry averages and historical operations to assess reasonableness and explain any significant variations.

(b) Collateral.

(1) Collateral must have documented value sufficient to protect the interest of the lender and the agency and, except as set forth in paragraph (b)(2) of this section, the discounted collateral value will normally be at least equal to the loan amount. Lenders will discount collateral consistent with sound loan-to-value policy.

(2) Some businesses are predominantly cash flow oriented, and where cash flow and profitability are strong, loan-to-value coverage may be discounted accordingly. A loan primarily based on cash flow must be supported by a successful and documented financial history.

(3) Do not reject B&I applications automatically when weak collateral is the only unfavorable factor. Other factors, such

as a strong indication of repayment ability and managerial ability, can offset this deficiency.

(4) Make sure that all worthwhile collateral is pledged to the project, but do not require assets with little or no collateral support to be pledged mainly for cosmetic reasons.

(c) Industry. Current status of the industry will be considered and businesses in areas of decline will be required to provide strong business plans which outline how they differ from the current trends. The regulatory environment surrounding the particular business or industry will be considered.

(d) Equity.

(1) A minimum of 10 percent tangible balance sheet equity will be required for existing businesses at loan closing. A minimum of 20 percent tangible balance sheet equity will be required for new businesses at loan closing. For energy projects, the minimum tangible balance sheet equity requirement range will be between 25 percent and 40 percent. Criteria for considering the minimum equity required for an individual application will be based on: existing businesses with successful financial and management history vs. start-up businesses; personal/corporate guarantees offered; contractual relationships with suppliers and buyers; credit rating; and strength of the business plan/feasibility study. Where the application is a request to refinance outstanding federal direct or guaranteed loans, without any new financing, the equity requirement may be determined using adjusted tangible net worth. An application that combines a refinancing guarantee request with a new loan guarantee request is subject to the standard, unadjusted, equity requirement except as provided in paragraphs (d)(1)(i) or (d)(1)(ii) of this section. Increases

or decreases in the equity requirements may be imposed or granted as follows: (Revised 07-26-06, PN 400.)

(i) A reduction in the equity requirement for existing businesses may be permitted by the Administrator. In order for a reduction to be considered, the borrower must furnish the following:

(A) Collateralized personal and corporate guarantees, including any parent, subsidiary, or affiliated company, when feasible and legally permissible (in accordance with **§ 4279.149 of this subpart), and**

(B) Pro forma and historical financial statements that indicate the business to be financed meets or exceeds the median quartile (as identified in Risk Management Association's Annual Statement Studies or similar publication) for the current ratio, quick ratio, debt-to-worth ratio, debt coverage ratio, and working capital.

(ii) The approval official may require more than the minimum equity requirements provided in this paragraph if the official makes a written determination that special circumstances necessitate this course of action.

(2) The equity requirement must be met in the form of either cash or tangible earning assets contributed to the business and reflected on the balance sheet. For sole proprietorships, financial statements should be prepared using only the assets and liabilities directly attributable to the business. Additionally, personal financial statements typically list assets at market values. The business assets must be valued at the lower of cost or market value before calculating tangible balance

sheet equity. Related party receivables routinely are classified as non-current assets, unless they will be repaid within one year. These receivables do not represent a liquid asset convertible to cash and available for business operations because of the nature of the affiliation and the absence of pressure to repay the receivables. The loan specialist should determine why the receivable was incurred and that repayment ability exists. Most banks deduct any amount due from officers or partners from total equity. For example, an officer may have taken a loan from the company instead of a salary or bonus. This receivable is, in effect, an expense not recognized by the company, thus improving its profitability. As a prudent lending practice, the agency must make the appropriate adjustment in the event the lender does not. Obtain a copy of any applicable promissory note to document collectability.

(3) The lender must certify that the equity requirement was determined using balance sheets prepared in accordance with GAAP and met upon giving effect to the entirety of the loan in the calculation, whether or not the loan itself is fully advanced, as of the date the guaranteed loan is closed. The final Loan Agreement must contain all conditions of the Conditional Commitment, including the tangible balance sheet equity requirement. Therefore, the business must meet the requirement before the lender executes the final loan documents and closes the loan. The lender must provide a certification to the Agency that tangible balance sheet equity was calculated from financial statements presented in accordance with GAAP and supported by attaching a copy of the balance sheet on which the certification is based.

(4) The agency may require higher equity requirements if conditions warrant. As a loan officer, you will expect to see tangible balance sheet equity meeting at least the minimum

requirement unless an exception is granted by the administrator. Riskier loans such as startups, recreation and tourism projects, energy-related businesses and loans without personal guarantees may necessitate a higher equity requirement than the minimum equity requirements noted above. Solid equity positions provide incentive for principals to remain committed to the success of the applicant while reducing the debt burden.

(e) Lien priorities. The entire loan will be secured by the same security with equal lien priority for the guaranteed and unguaranteed portions of the loan. The unguaranteed portion of the loan will neither be paid first nor given any preference or priority over the guaranteed portion. A parity or junior position may be considered provided that discounted collateral values are adequate to secure the loan in accordance with paragraph (b) of this section after considering prior liens.

(f) Management. A thorough review of key management personnel will be completed to ensure that the business has adequately trained and experienced managers. Assessment of management in areas such as education, experience, and motivation is an important factor in loan analysis. Consider the lender's opinion on management, but do your own independent assessment and document your findings in the loan docket. Comment briefly when management capacity is clearly satisfactory. Otherwise, address any weaknesses and document measures to bolster deficient areas. Work closely with the lender if there are concerns in the management of the business.

B&I EXCERPT 12

§ 4279.143 Insurance

(a) Hazard. Hazard insurance with a standard mortgage clause naming the lender as beneficiary will be required on every loan in an amount that is at least the lesser of the depreciated replacement value of the collateral or the amount of the loan. Hazard insurance includes fire, windstorm, lightning, hail, explosion, riot, civil commotion, aircraft, vehicle, marine, smoke, builder's risk during construction by the business, and property damage.

(b) Life. The lender may require life insurance to insure against the risk of death of persons critical to the success of the business. When required, coverage will be in amounts necessary to provide for management succession or to protect the business. The cost of insurance and its effect on the applicant's working capital must be considered as well as the amount of existing insurance which could be assigned without requiring additional expense.

(c) Worker compensation. Worker compensation insurance is required in accordance with State law.

(d) Flood. National flood insurance is required in accordance with 7 CFR, part 1806, subpart B (RD Instruction 426.2, available in any field office or the National Office).

(e) Other. Public liability, business interruption, malpractice, and other insurance appropriate to the borrower's particular business and circumstances will be considered and required when needed to protect the interests of the borrower.

§ 4279.144 APPRAISALS

Lenders will be responsible for ensuring that appraisal values adequately reflect the actual value of the collateral. All real property appraisals associated with agency guaranteed loan making and servicing transactions will meet the requirements contained in the Financial Institutions Reform, Recovery and Enforcement Act (FIRREA) of 1989 and the appropriate guidelines contained in Standards 1 and 2 of the Uniform Standards of Professional Appraisal Practices (USPAP). In accordance with USPAP, the agency will require documentation that the appraiser has the necessary experience and competency to appraise the property in question. All appraisals will include consideration of the potential effects from a release of hazardous substances or petroleum products or other environmental hazards on the market value of the collateral. To protect the interest of the lender and agency, the lender should complete and submit its technical review of the appraisal. For additional guidance and information concerning the completion of real property appraisals, refer to "Standard Practices for Environmental Site Assessments: Transaction Screen Questionnaire" and "Phase I Environmental Site Assessment," both published by the American Society of Testing and Materials. Chattels will be evaluated in accordance with normal banking practices and generally accepted methods of determining value. (Revised 10-26-11, PN 452.)

B&I EXCERPT 13

§ 4279.149 Personal and corporate guarantees (Revised 05-16-07, PN 409)

(a) Unconditional personal and corporate guarantees are part of the collateral for the loan, but are not considered in determining whether a loan is adequately secured for loan making purposes. Agency approved personal and corporate guarantees for the full term of the loan and at least equal to the guarantor's percent interest in the borrower, times the loan amount are required from those owning at least 20 percent interest in the borrower, unless the lender documents to the agency's satisfaction that collateral, equity, cash flow, and profitability indicate an above-average ability to repay the loan. The guarantors will execute Form RD 4279-14, "Unconditional Guarantee." A signature section must be created and in accordance with applicable law. The signature block must include the legal name of the individual or entity signing the guarantee and, where applicable, the name and title of the authorized representative who will execute the document on its behalf. For instructions on how to complete an enforceable signature block that complies with applicable state law, consult with the regional attorney. When warranted by an agency assessment of potential financial risk, agency approved guarantees may also be required of parent, subsidiaries, or affiliated companies (owning less than a 20 percent interest in the borrower) and require security for any guarantee provided under this section.

Exceptions to the requirement for personal guarantees must be requested by the lender and concurred by the agency approval official on a case-by-case basis. The lender must document that collateral, equity, cash flow, and profitability indicate an above-average ability to repay the loan. Closely review collateral, equity, cash flow, and profitability before concurring in any exception to guarantees.

B&I EXCERPT 14

§ 4279.150 Feasibility studies

A feasibility study by a qualified independent consultant may be required by the agency for start-up businesses or existing businesses when the project will significantly affect the borrower's operations. An acceptable feasibility study should include, but not be limited to, economic, market, technical, financial, and management feasibility. Feasibility studies will normally be conducted in accordance with Appendix A of this subpart.

B&I EXCERPT 15

§ 4279.166 Timeframe for processing applications.

All guaranteed loan applications should be approved or disapproved, and the lender notified in writing not later than sixty days after receipt of a completed application, unless approval is prevented by lack of guarantee authority.

> (a) If an application is not complete, the lender will be notified in writing not later than twenty days after receipt of the application by the agency of the reasons the application is incomplete.

> (b) When an application is disapproved, the written notification to the lender will state the reasons for disapproval and appropriate appeal rights will be provided.

B&I EXCERPT 16

§ 4279.173 Loan approval and obligating funds

> (a) Upon approval of a loan guarantee, the agency will issue a conditional commitment to the lender containing conditions under which a loan note guarantee will be issued.

> (b) If certain conditions of the conditional commitment cannot be met, the lender and applicant may propose alternate conditions. Within the requirements of the applicable regulations and instructions and prudent lending practices, the agency

may negotiate with the lender and the applicant regarding any proposed changes to the conditional commitment.

(c) The conditional commitment is a key processing step in the B&I process. The conditional commitment should be issued to the lender and borrower on or after the obligation date. You should tailor each conditional commitment to the project and ensure that the lender understands each item. All required measures identified in the agency's environmental assessment for this proposal and established for the purpose of avoiding or reducing adverse environmental impacts of the proposal's construction or operation must be listed in the conditional commitment and understood by both the lender and the borrower. Requirements of the conditional commitment, including the equity requirement, must be incorporated into the loan agreement in accordance with § 4279.161(b)(11)(xii). (Revised 03-23-05, PN 384)

(d) Make sure that the lender understands that the agency expects strong servicing of the loan and that the agency will, except in the case of delinquencies and liquidations, play a very minimal servicing role. The lender should service the loan the way it does any loan in its portfolio. Make lenders aware of the ramifications of negligent servicing.

(e) The national office will review a sample of loans based on the number of loans approved by the state office. Failure to submit these reviews when requested by the national office could result in suspension of loan approval authority. Upon request by the national office, the entire case file will be submitted to the attention of the Director, B&I Division. (Revised 11-18-10, PN 443)

Appendix B

USDA COMMUNITY FACILITIES GUARANTEED LOAN PROGRAM

Complete instructions regarding the USDA Community Facilities Guaranteed Loan Program can be found at:

- RD 1942A: http://www.rurdev.usda.gov/wa/Program%20PDF/CF%20CONFORMS/1%20RD%20Instruction%201942-A%20with%20All%20Guides%20and%20Attachmentspdf.pdf

Below are key excerpts we think you will find helpful.

CF EXCERPT 1

§1942.17 Community Facilities

(a) General. This section includes information and procedures specifically designed for use by applicants, including their professional consultants and/or agents who provide such assistance and services as architectural, engineering, financial, legal, or other services related to application processing and facility planning and development. This section is made available as needed for such use. It includes Rural Development policies and requirements pertaining to loans for community facilities. It provides applicants with guidance for usein proceeding with their application. Rural Development shall cooperate fully with appropriate State agencies to give maximum support of the State's strategies for development of rural areas. (Revised 05-19-92, SPECIAL PN)

(b) Eligibility. Financial assistance to areas or communities adjacent to, or closely associated with, non-rural areas is limited by §1942.17 (c) of this subpart. (Revised 05-19-92, SPECIAL PN)

(1) Applicant.

(i) A public body, such as a municipality, county, district, authority, or other political subdivision of a state.

(A) Loans for water or waste disposal facilities will not be made to a city or town with a population in excess of 10,000 inhabitants, according to the latest decennialcensus of the United States.

(B) Loans for essential community facilities will not be made to a city or town with a population in excess of 20,000 inhabitants, according to the latest decennialcensus of the United States.

(ii) An organization operated on a not-for-profit basis, such as an association, cooperative, or private corporation. Applicants organized under the general profit corporation laws may be eligible if they actually will be operated on a not-for-profitbasis under their charter, bylaws, mortgage, or supplemental agreement provisions as may be required as a condition of loan approval. Essential community facility applicants other than utility-type must have significant ties with the local rural community. Such ties are necessary to ensure to the greatest extent possible that a facility under private control will carry out a public purpose and continue to primarily serve rural areas. Ties may be evidenced by items such as:

(A) Association with or controlled by a local public body or bodies, or broadly based ownership and controlled by members of the community.

(B) Substantial public funding through taxes, revenue bonds, or other local Government sources, and/or substantial voluntary community funding, such as would be obtained through a community-wide funding campaign.

(iii) Indian tribes on federal and state reservations and other federally recognized Indian tribes.

(2) Facility.

(i) Facilities must be located in rural areas, except for utility-type services such as water, sewer, natural gas, or hydroelectric, serving both rural and non-rural areas. In such cases, Rural Development funds may be used to finance only that portion serving rural areas, regardless of facility location.

(ii) Essential community facilities must primarily serve rural areas.

(iii) For water or waste disposal facilities, the terms "rural" and "rural area" will not include any area in any city or town with a population in excess of 10,000 inhabitants, according to the latest decennial census of the United States.

(iv) For essential community facilities, the terms "rural" and "rural area" will not include any area in any city or town with a population in excess of 20,000 inhabitants, according to the latest decennial census of the United States.

(3) Credit elsewhere. Applicants must certify in writing and Rural Development shall determine and document that the applicant is unable to finance the proposed project from their own resources or through commercial credit at reasonable rates and terms.

(4) Legal authority and responsibility. Each applicant must have or will obtain the legal authority necessary for constructing operating and maintaining the proposed facility or service and for obtaining giving security for and repaying the proposed loan. Theapplicant shall be responsible for operating maintaining and managing the facility and providing for its continued availability and use at reasonable rates and terms. This responsibility shall be exercised by the applicant even though the facility may be operated maintained or managed by a third party under contract management agreement or written lease. Leases may be used when this is the only feasible way to provide the service and is the customary practice. Management agreements should provide for at least those items listed in Guide 24 of this subpart (available in any agency office). Such contracts management agreements or leases must not contain options or other provisions for transfer of ownership.

(5) Refinancing debt. The government shall require an agreement that if at any time it shall appear to the government that the borrower is able to refinance the amount of the indebtedness then outstanding in whole or in part by obtaining a loan for such purposes from responsible cooperative or private credit sources at reasonable rates and terms for loans for similar purposes and periods of time the borrower will upon request of the government apply for and accept such loan in sufficient amount to repay the government and will

take all such actions as may be required in connection with such loan.

(6) Expanded eligibility for timber-dependent communities in Pacific Northwest. In the Pacific Northwest defined as an area containing national forest covered by the federal document entitled Forest Plan for a Sustainable Economy and a Sustainable Environment, dated July 1, 1993; the population limits contained §1942.17(b) are expanded to include communities with not more than 25,000 inhabitants until September 30, 1998 if: (Added 09-06-95, PN 250)

(i) Part or all of the community lies within 100 miles of the boundary of a national forest covered by the federal document entitled Forest Plan for a Sustainable Economy and a Sustainable Environment, dated July 1, 1993; and

(ii) The community is located in a county in which at least 15 percent of the total primary and secondary labor and proprietor income is derived from forestry, wood products, or forest-related industries such as recreation and tourism.

CF EXCERPT 2

§1942.17 Community Facilities (cont.)

(d) Eligible loan purposes.

(1) Funds may be used:

(i) To construct, enlarge, extend, or otherwise improve water or waste disposal and other essential community facilities providing essential service primarily to rural residents and rural businesses. Rural businesses would include facilities such as educational and other publicly owned facilities. (Revised 05-19-92, SPECIAL PN.)

(A) "Water or waste disposal facilities" include water, sanitary sewerage, solid waste disposal, and storm wastewater facilities.

(B) "Essential community facilities" are those public improvements requisite to the beneficial and orderly development of a community operated on a nonprofit basis including but not limited to: (Revised 11-4-87, PN 68)

(1) Health services;

(2) Community, social, or cultural services;

(3) Transportation facilities, such as streets, roads, and bridges;

(4) Hydroelectric generating facilities and related connecting systems and appurtenances, when not eligible for Rural Electrification Administration(REA) financing;

(5) Supplemental and supporting structures for other rural electrification or telephone systems (including facilities such as headquarters and office buildings, storage facilities, and maintenance shops) when not eligible for Rural Electrification Administration financing:

(6) Natural gas distribution systems; and

(7) Industrial park sites, but only to the extent of land acquisition and necessary site preparation, including access ways and utility extensions to andthroughout

the site. Funds may not be used in connection with industrial parks to finance on-site utility systems, or business and industrial buildings.

(C) "Otherwise improve" includes but is not limited to the following:

(1) The purchase of major equipment, such as solid waste collection trucks, and X-ray machines, which will in themselves provide an essential service to rural residents (Revised 11-4-87, PN 68)

(2) The purchase of existing facilities when it is necessary either to Iimprove or to prevent a loss of service;

(3) Payment of tap fees and other utility connection charges as provided in utility purchase contracts prepared under section 1942.18(f) of this subpart.

(ii) To construct or relocate public buildings, roads, bridges, fences, or utilities, and to make other public improvements necessary to the successful operation or protection of facilities authorized in paragraph (d)(l)(i) of this section.

(iii) To relocate private buildings, roads, bridges, fences, or utilities, and other private improvements necessary to the successful operation or protection of facilities authorized in paragraph (d)(l)(i) of this section.

(iv) To pay the following expenses, but only when such expenses are a necessary part of a loan to finance facilities authorized in paragraphs (d)(l)(i), (d)(l)(ii), and (d)(l)(iii) of this section:

(A) Reasonable fees and costs such as legal, engineering, architectural, fiscal advisory, recording, environmental impact analyses, archaeological surveys and possible salvage or other mitigation measures, planning, establishing or acquiring rights.

(B) Interest on loans until the facility is self supporting, but not for more than three years unless a longer period is approved by the national office; interest on loans secured by general obligation bonds until tax revenues are available for payment, but not for more than two years unless a longer period is approved by the national office; and interest on interim financing, including interest charges on interim financing from sources other than Rural Development.

(C) Costs of acquiring interest in land; rights, such as water rights, leases, permits, rights-of-way; and other evidence of land or water control necessary for development of the facility.

(D) Purchasing or renting equipment necessary to install, maintain, extend, protect, operate, or utilize facilities.

(E) Initial operating expenses for a period ordinarily not exceeding one year when the borrower is unable to pay such expenses.

(F) Refinancing debts incurred by, or on behalf of, a community when all of the following conditions exist:

> (1) The debts being refinanced are a secondary part of the total loan;
>
> (2) The debts are incurred for the facility or service being financed or any part thereof;

(3) Arrangements cannot be made with the creditors to extend or modify the terms of the debts so that a sound basis will exist for making a loan.

(G) Prepay costs for which Rural Development grant funds were obligated provided there is:

(1) No conflict with the loan resolution, state statutes, or any other loan requirements; and

(2) Full documentation showing that:

(i) Loan funds will only be utilized on a temporary basis; and

(ii) All Rural Development loan funds are restored at a later date for purpose(s) for which they were obligated.

(v) To pay obligations for construction incurred before loan approval. Construction work should not be started and obligations for such work or materials should not be incurred before the loan is approved. However, if there are compelling reasons for proceeding with construction before loan approval, applicants may request Rural Development approval to pay such obligations. Such requests may be approved if Rural Development determines that:

(A) Compelling reasons exist for incurring obligations before loan approval; and

(B) The obligations will be incurred for authorized loan purposes; and

(C) Contract documents have been approved by Rural Development; and

(D) All environmental requirements applicable to Rural Development and the applicant have been met; and

(E) The applicant has the legal authority to incur the obligations at the time proposed, and payment of the debts will remove any basis for any mechanic, material or other liens that may attach to the security property. Rural Development may authorize payment of such obligations at the time of loan closing. Rural Development's authorization to pay such obligations, however, is on the condition that it is not committed to make the loan; it assumes no responsibility for any obligations incurred by the applicant; and the applicant must subsequently meet all loan approval requirements. The applicant's request and Rural Development authorization for paying such obligations shall be in writing. If construction is started without Rural Development approval, post approval in accordance with this section may be considered.

(2) Funds may not be used to finance:

(i) On-site utility systems or business and industrial buildings in connection with industrial parks.

(ii) Facilities to be used primarily for recreation purposes.

(iii) Community antenna television services or facilities.

(iv) Electric generation or transmission facilities or telephone systems, except as provided in paragraph (d)(1)(i)(B)(4) or (d)(1)(i)(B)(5) of this section; or extensions to serve a particular essential community facility as provided in paragraph (d)(1)(ii) or (d)(1)(iii) of this section. (Revised 11-4-87, PN 68.)

(v) Facilities that are not modest in size, design, and cost.

(vi) Loan or grant finder's fees.

(vii) Projects located within the Coastal Barriers Resource System that do not qualify for an exception as defined in Section 6 of the Coastal Barriers Resource Act, P.L. 97-348.

(viii) New combined sanitary and storm water sewer facilities.

(ix) That portion of a water and/or waste disposal facility normally provided by a business or industrial user. (Added 05- 19-92, SPECIAL PN.)

CF EXCERPT 3

§1942.17 (e) (5) Community Facilities (cont.)

(f) Rates and terms.

(1) General. Each loan will bear interest at the rate prescribed in RD Instruction 440.1, Exhibit B (available in any Rural Development office). The interest rates will be set by Rural Development at least for each quarter of the fiscal year. All rates will be adjusted to the nearest one-eighth of one percent. For each loan, the basis for determining what interest rate is appropriate will be completely documented on the automated Community Facilities Project Summary. The applicant may submit a written request prior to loan closing that the interest rate charged on the loan be thelower of the rate in effect at the time of loan approval or the rate in effect at the time of loan closing. If the interest rate is to be that in effect at loan closing, the interest rate charged on a loan involving multiple advances of Rural Development funds, using temporary debt instruments, shall be that in effect on the date when the first temporary debt instrument is issued.

If no written request is received from the applicant prior to loan closing, the interest rate charged on the loan will be the rate in effect at the time of loan approval. (Revised 03-19-03, PN 357)

CF EXCERPT 4

§1942.17 (f) Community Facilities (cont.)

(7) Repayment terms. The loan repayment period shall not exceed the useful life of the facility, State statute or forty years from the date of the note(s) or bond(s), whichever is less. Where Rural Development grant funds are used in connection with an Rural Development loan, the loan will be for the maximum term permitted by this subpart, state statute, or the useful life of the facility, whichever is less, unless there is an exceptional case where circumstances justify making an Rural Development loan for less than the maximum term permitted. In such cases, the reasons must befully documented. In all cases, including those in which the Rural Development is jointly financing with another lender, the Rural Development payments of principal and interest should approximate amortized installments. (Revised 06-26-91, PN 168.)

(i) Principal payments may be deferred, in whole or in part, for a period not to exceed thirty-six months following the date the first interest installment is due. If for any reason it appears necessary to permit a longer period of deferment, the state director may authorize such deferment with the prior approval of the national office. Deferments of principal will not be used to: (Revised and Renumbered 03-01-88, SPECIAL PN)

(A) Postpone the levying of taxes or assessments.

(B) Delay collection of the full rates, which the borrower has agreed to charge users for its services as soon as major benefits or the improvements are available to those users.

(C) Create reserves for normal operation and maintenance.

(D) Make any capital improvements except those approved by Rural Development determined to be essential to the repayment of the loan or to the obtaining of adequate security thereof.

(E) Accelerate the payment of other debts.

(ii) Payment date. Loan payments will be scheduled to coincide with income availability and be in accordance with state law. If consistent with the foregoing, monthly payments will be required and will be enumerated in the bond, otherevidence of indebtedness, or other supplemental agreement. However, if state law only permits principal plus interest (P&I) type bonds, annual or semi-annual payments will be used. Insofar as practical monthly payments will be scheduled one full month following the date of loan closing; or semiannual or annual payments will be scheduled six or twelve full months respectively, following the date of loan closing or any deferment period. Due dates falling on the 29th, 30th or 31st day of the month will be avoided. (Revised 06-26-91, PN 168.)

(g) Security. Loans will be secured by the best security position practicable in a manner, which will adequately protect the interest of Rural Development during the repayment period of the loan. Specific requirements for security for each loan will be included in a letter of conditions.

CF EXCERPT 5

§1942.17 (g) (2) Community Facilities (cont.)

(iii) Other essential community facilities other than utility type, such as those for public health and safety, social, and cultural needs and the like will meet the following security requirements:

(A) Such loans will be secured by one or a combination of the following and in the following order of preference:

(1) General obligation bonds.

(2) Assessments.

(3) Bonds that pledge other taxes.

(4) Bonds pledging revenues of the facility being financed when such bonds provide for the mandatory levy and collection of taxes in the event revenues later become insufficient to properly operate and maintain the facility and to retire the loan.

(5) Assignment of assured income that will be available for the life of the loan, from such sources as insurance premium rebates, income from endowments, irrevocable trusts, or commitments from industries, public bodies, or other reliable sources.

(6) Liens on real and chattel property when legally permissible and an assignment of the borrowers income from applicants who have been in existence and are able to present evidence of a financially successful operation of a similar facility for a period of time sufficient to indicate project success. National office concurrence

is required when the applicant has been in existence for less than five years or has not operated on a financially successful basis for five years immediately prior to loan application.

(7) Liens on real and chattel property when legally permissible and an assignment of income from an organization receiving Health and Human Services (HHS) operating grants under the "Memorandum of understanding Between Health Resources and Services Administration, U. S. Department of Health and Human Services and Rural Development, U. S. Department of Agriculture" (see RD Instruction 2000-T, available in any Rural Development office)

(8) Liens on real and chattel property when legally permissible and an assignment of income from an organization proposing a facility whose users receive reliable income from programs such as socialsecurity, supplemental security income (SSI), retirement plans, long-term insurance annuities, Medicare or Medicaid. Examples are homes for the handicapped or institutions whose clientele receive State or local governmentassistance.

(9) When the applicant cannot meet the criteria in paragraph (g)(2)(iii)(A)(1) through (8) of this section, such proposals may be considered when all the following are met:

(i) The applicant is a new organization or one that has not operated the type of facility being proposed.

(ii) There is a demonstration of exceptional community support such as substantial financial contributions, and aggressive leadership in theformation of the organization and proposed project, which indicates a commitment of the entire community.

(iii) The state director has determined that adequate and dependable revenues will be available to meet all operation expenses, debtrepayment, and the required reserve.

(iv) Prior national office review and concurrence is obtained.

(B) Real estate and chattel property taken as security in accordance with paragraphs (g)(2)(iii)(A)(6) through (9) of this section:

(1) Ordinarily will include the property that is used in connection with the facility being financed; and

(2) Will have an as-developed present market value determined by a qualified appraiser equal to or exceeding the amount of the loan to be obtained plus any other indebtedness against the proposed security; and

(3) May have one of the lien requirements deleted when the loan approval official determines that the loan will be adequately secured with a lien on either the real estate or chattel property.

(C) When security is not available in accordance with paragraphs (g)(2)(iii)(A)(1) through (5) of this section and State law precludes securing the loan with liens on real or chattel property, the loan will be secured in thebest manner consistent with State law and customary security taken by private lenders in the State, such as revenue bonds, and any other security the loan approval official determines necessary for a sound loan. Such loans will otherwise meet the requirements of (g)(2)(iii)(A)(6) through (9) of this section as appropriate.

CF EXCERPT 6

§1942.17 (g)(3)(iii)(A)(5)

(h) Economic feasibility requirements. All projects financed under the provisions of this section must be based on taxes, assessments, revenues, fees or other satisfactory sources of revenues in an amount sufficient to provide for facility operation and maintenance, areasonable reserve, and debt payment. An overall review of the applicant's financial status, including a review of all assets and liabilities, will be a part of the docket review process by the Rural Development staff and approval official. If the primary use of thefacility is by business and the success or failure of the facility is dependent on the business, then the economic viability of that business must be assessed. The number of users for a rural business will be based on equivalent dwelling units, which is the level of service provided to a typical rural residential dwelling. (Revised 05-19-92, SPECIAL PN)

(1) Financial feasibility reports. All applicants will be expected to provide a financial feasibility report prepared by a qualified firm or individual. These financial feasibility reports will normally be:

(i) Included as part of the preliminary engineer/ architectural report using Guides 6 through 10 as applicable; or

(ii) Prepared by a qualified firm or individual not having a direct interest in the management or construction of the facility using Guide 5 when:

(A) The project will significantly affect the applicant's financial operations and is not a utility-type facility but is dependent on revenues from the facility to repay the loan; or

(B) It is specifically requested by Rural Development.

(2) Applicants for loans for utility-type facilities dependent on users fees for debt payment shall base their income and expense forecast on realistic user estimates in accordance with the following:

(i) In estimating the number of users and establishing rates or fees on which the loan will be based for new systems and for extensions or improvements to existing systems, consideration should be given to the following:

(A) An estimated number of maximum initial users should not be used when setting user fees and rates since it may be several years before all residents in the community will need the services provided by the system. In establishing rates a realistic number of initial users should be employed.

(B) User agreements from individual vacant property owners will not be considered when determining project feasibility unless:

(1) The owner has plans to develop the property in a reasonable period of time and become a user of the facility; and

(2) The owner agrees in writing to make a monthly payment at least equal to the proportionate share of debt service attributable to the vacant property until the property is developed and the facility is utilized on

a regular basis. A bond or escrowed security deposit must be provided to guarantee this monthly payment and to guarantee an amount at leastequal to the owner's proportionate share of construction costs. If a bond is provided, it must be executed by a surety company that appears on theTreasury Department's most current list (Circular 570, as amended) and be authorized to transact business in the State where the project is located. The guarantee shall be payable jointly to the borrower and Rural Development; and

(3) Such guarantee will mature not later than four years from the date of execution and will be finally due and payable upon default of a monthly payment or at maturity, unless the property covered by the guarantee has been developed and the facility is being utilized on a regular basis.

(C) Income from other vacant property owners will be considered only as extra income.

(ii) Realistic user estimates will be established as follows:

(A) Meaningful potential user cash contributions. Potential user cash contributions are required except:

(1) For users presently receiving service, or

(2) Where Rural Development determines that the potential users as a whole in the applicant's service area cannot make cash contributions, or

(3) Where State statutes or local ordinances require mandatory use of the system and the applicant or legal entity having such authority agrees in writing to enforce such statutes, or ordinances.

(B) The amount of cash contributions required in paragraph (h)(2)(ii)(A) of this section will be set by the applicant and concurred in by Rural Development. Contributions should be an amount high enough to indicate sincere interest on the part of the potential user, but not so high as to preclude service to low-income families. Contributions ordinarily should be an amount approximating one year's minimum user fee, and shall be paid in full before loan closing or commencement of construction, whichever occurs first. Once economic feasibility is ascertained based on a demonstration of meaningful potential user cash contributions, the contribution, membership fee or other fees that may be imposed are not a requirement of Rural Development under this section. However, borrowers do have an additional responsibility relating to generating sufficient revenues as set forth in paragraph (n)(2)(iii) of this section.

(C) Enforceable user agreement. Except for users presently receiving service, an enforceable user agreement with a penalty clause is required unless state statutes or local ordinances require mandatory use of the system and the applicant or legal entity having such authority agrees in writing to enforce such statutes or ordinances.

(iii) In those cases where all or part of the borrower's debt payment revenues will come from user fees, applicants must provide a positive program to encourage connection by all users as soon as service is available. The program will be available for review and approval by Rural Development before loan closing or commencement of construction, whichever occurs first. Such a program shall include:

(A) An aggressive information program to be carried out during the construction period. The borrower should send written notification to all signed users at least three weeks in advance of the date service will be available, stating the date users will be expected to have their connections completed, and the date user charges will begin.

(B) Positive steps to assure that installation services will be available. These may be provided by the contractor installing the system, local plumbingcompanies, or local contractors.

(C) Aggressive action to see that all signed users can finance their connections. This might require collection of sufficient user contributions to finance connections. Extreme cases might necessitate additional loan funds for this purpose; however, loan funds should be used only when absolutely necessary and when approved by Rural Development prior to loan closing.

Appendix C

USDA GUARANTEED LOAN PROGRAM DEFAULT, PROTECTIVE ADVANCES, AND LIQUIDATION REGULATION

4287.145—Default

1. Lender notifies USDA when borrower is thirty days past due.

    a. Lender submits 1980-44 bimonthly

2. If borrower is sixty days past due, lender will schedule a meeting with agency and borrower to resolve the problem

Options to cure loan

1. Deferment of principal (subject to right of holder)
2. An additional unguaranteed temporary loan by lender to bring the account current
3. Re-amortization of the payments (subject to right of holder) will be limited to the remaining life of collateral
4. Transfer and assumption of the loan in accordance with 4287.134
5. Reorganization

6. Liquidation

7. Subsequent loan guarantees

8. Change in interest rate (with holders approval)

Protective Advances

1. Agency written authorization is required on cumulative protective advances over $5,000

2. Protective advances include but are not limited to

    a. Property taxes

    b. Annual assessments

    c. Ground rent

    d. Hazard or flood insurance premiums

    e. Other expenses necessary to preserve or protect the security

RD will pay half of the liquidation appraisal.

*Attorney fees are not a protective advance.

4287.157—Liquidation

1. Decisions to liquidate

    a. Loan has been delinquent ninety days

    b. Delaying liquidation will jeopardize full recovery of loan

    c. Borrower or lender has been uncooperative

2. Liquidation by lender

      a. Lender will, within thirty days after a decision to liquidate, must submit in writing proposed, detailed method of liquidation

3. Lenders liquidation plan 4287.157(d) (1-13)

4. Approval of liquidation plan

      a. Within 30 days after receipt of the liquidation plan, the agency will inform the lender in writing whether it concurs.

      *When the liquidation plan is approved by the agency, the lender will proceed expeditiously with liquidation

5. Acceleration

      a. The lender will proceed to accelerate the indebtedness as expeditiously as possible

      b. A copy of the acceleration letter of documents will be sent to the agency

6. Estimated loss claim

      a. Lender will file an estimated loss claim once a decision has been made to liquidate if the liquidation will exceed ninety days.

      b. Lender will discontinue interest accrual after the estimated loss claim if filed (ninety days).

7. Lender reports to agency

      a. When lender conducts liquidation it will account for funds during the period of liquidation and will provide the agency with reports at least quarterly on the progress of the liquidation.

8. Final Report of loss

   a. Final loss—within thirty days after liquidation of all collateral a final report of loss must be prepared and submitted by the lender to the agency.

   b. The agency will not guarantee interest beyond this thirty-day period other than for the period of time it takes the agency to process the loss claim.

   c. Loss payment will be paid by the agency within sixty days after the review of the final loss report and accounting of the collateral.

Appendix D

RD 1980-41

FORM APPROVED OMB NO. 0670-0016

USDA-RD Form RD 1980-41 (Rev. 12-99)	UNITED STATES DEPARTMENT OF AGRICULTURE RURAL DEVELOPMENT **GUARANTEED LOAN STATUS REPORT**	AS OF DATE MO DA YR

INSTRUCTIONS TO LENDER - COMPLETE PART B AS APPLICABLE

PART A - IDENTIFYING INFORMATION - See Reverse

1. BORROWER ID NBR	2. AGENCY LOAN NBR	3. LENDER LOAN NBR	4. BORROWER NAME
5. LOAN TYPE		6. LENDER INT RATE GUARANTEED	7. LENDER INT RATE NONGUARANTEED
8. DATE OF LAST STATUS UPDATE		9. DATE OF LOAN	10. LOAN AMOUNT

PART B - TO BE COMPLETED BY LENDER

11. UNPAID PRINCIPAL $	12. UNPAID INTEREST $	13. AMOUNT ADVANCED DURING THE CURRENT REPORTING PERIOD $
14. LENDER INT RATE GUARANTEED		15. LENDER INT RATE NONGUARANTEED
16. PAYMENT STATUS CODE A=Borrower Ahead of Schedule B=Borrower Behind Schedule C=Borrower Current	17. AMOUNT AHEAD OR BEHIND SCHEDULE $	18. TERMINATE GUARANTEE Y=Terminate N=Do not Terminate

19. IF THE BORROWER IS BEHIND SCHEDULE, PLEASE INDICATE WHAT IS BEING DONE TO BRING THE ACCOUNT CURRENT.

20. PLEASE SUBMIT THE ORIGINAL OF THIS REPORT WITHIN 30 DAYS TO	21. AUTHORIZED LENDER SIGNATURE X
	22. TITLE
	23. DATE

24. LENDER NAME AND ADDRESS	IF THE LENDER INFORMATION IN ITEM 24 IS IN ERROR, PLEASE SHOW CORRECTIONS HERE.
	LNDR ID LNDR BRCH

According to the Paperwork Reduction Act of 1995, no persons are required to respond to a collection of information unless it displays a valid OMB control number. The valid OMB control number for this information collection is 0570-0016. The time required to complete this information collection is estimated to average 20 minutes per response, including the time for reviewing instructions, searching existing data sources, gathering and maintaining the data needed, and completing and reviewing the collection of information.

Appendix E

SAMPLE OF FARMERMACII, LLC SECONDARY MARKET FOR USDA GUARANTEED LOANS WEEKLY RATE LINE

FARMERMAC II LLC
Secondary Market for USDA Guaranteed Loans

IMPORTANT

Rate Line

- Servicing Retained Net Yields*

Posted: 2/26/2013 10:05 AM ET

Product Types	Monthly Pay Cash	Monthly Pay 4-Week Rate Lock	Annual, S.A., & Qrtly Pay Cash	Annual, S.A., & Qrtly Pay 4-Week Rate Lock
Wall Street Journal Prime **	1.75%		1.75%	
Farmer Mac 3-Mo COFI	1.46%		1.46%	
Farmer Mac 5-Yr Reset COFI, 20, 25, 30-Yr Am	1.89%	1.98%	1.99%	2.08%
Farmer Mac 10-Yr Reset COFI, 20, 25, 30-Yr Am	2.62%	2.71%	2.72%	2.81%
Farmer Mac 15-Yr Reset COFI, 20, 25, 30-Yr Am	3.05%	3.14%	3.15%	3.24%
7-Yr Fixed Rate, 7-Yr Am	1.83%	1.92%	1.93%	2.02%
7-Yr Fixed Rate, 15-Yr Am	2.05%	2.14%	2.15%	2.24%
10-Yr Fixed Rate, 10-Yr Am	2.37%	2.46%	2.47%	2.56%
15-Yr Fixed Rate, 15-Yr Am	2.67%	2.76%	2.77%	2.86%
15-Yr Fixed Rate, 25-Yr Am	2.96%	3.05%	3.06%	3.15%
20-Yr Fixed Rate, 20-Yr Am	2.99%	3.08%	3.09%	3.18%

* Indications only - actual Net Yields are determined at time of pricing and may differ from those indicated.
** For daily, monthly and quarterly resets. For all other reset frequencies, please contact Farmer Mac II LLC.

NOTE: Rates are set by Farmer Mac on behalf of Farmer Mac II LLC.

Term	Description
Loan Pricing	Loans receiving Cash Rates are priced each Wednesday. Rate locks are issued on Weekdays (10:00-3:00 ET) to registered lenders with pre-approved notes.
Settlement/Purchase	Farmer Mac II LLC purchases loans each Thursday. Loans should be delivered to Colson Services Corp. one week prior to the anticipated Settlement Date.
Eligible Loans	Farm Service Agency (FSA)- Farm Ownership (FO) & term Operating Loan (OL) Rural Development (RD)- Business & Industry (B&I) & Community Facility (CF)
Servicing Fees	Determined by the lender and added to the Net Yield. Lender is responsible for collecting, reporting, and remitting loan payments to Colson.
Prepayment	Borrower may prepay loan in part or in full at any time without penalty.
Next Reset Dates	3-Mo COFI- 4/1/2013 and quarterly thereafter 5-Yr Reset COFI- 1/1/2018 and every 5 years thereafter 10-Yr Reset COFI- 1/1/2023 and every 10 years thereafter 15-Yr Reset COFI- 1/1/2028 and every 15 years thereafter Balloons are not permitted on loans tied to either the 5-, 10- or 15- Year Reset COFI. Payments must adjust with rate changes to insure proper loan amortization.
Payment Options & Dates	Annual- January 1, April 1, July 1, or October 1 Semi-annual- January 1 & July 1, or April 1 & October 1 Quarterly- 1st day of each calendar quarter Monthly- 1st day of each month
Simple Interest	Preferred accrual method - A/365
Transaction/Origination Fees	All fees are included in the Net Yield. Lenders are free to charge origination points.

For more information, contact us at 877-770-FMII (3644) or visit www.farmermac2.com.

Appendix F

B&I AND CF INFORMATION CHECKLIST

Project: _____

Loan Package Requirements

Business Financial Requirments:				Required	Received
Description/History of business being financed, Federal ID #, Company Contact, with phone numbers and email address					
DUNS # (if the company doesn't have a DUNS# we can assist them obtaining it)					
Interim financial statement (month and year-to-date) - **within 30 days of current date**					
Business Debt Schedule (form attached), as of the same date as the interim financial statement					
Aging of accounts receivable and accounts payable as of the date of the interim financial					
Fiscal yearend business statements for prior three (3) years		2011			
		2010			
		2009			
Business federal tax returns for three prior years, to include supporting schedules and		2011			
If the most recent returns have not been filed a copy of the federal tax extension is required.		2010			
		2009			
Business Plan for new business or Strategic Plan for expansion plans describing the company and the project being financed.					
Income projections for the next three full years of operations from the date of the proposed loan, with the first year by month. Do not include interest expense.					
List of assets (land, building, equipment, inventory, accounts receivable etc...) being used as collateral with estimated current value or purchase cost.					
Organizational documents including Articles and By-Laws or Certificate of Organization, Operating Agreements					
Detailed ownership breakdown					

		Partner	Partner	Partner	Partner
Personal Financial Requirements: (Required for each partner owning 20% or more)					
Personal financial statement signed and dated within the last 30 days(if needed form attached)					
Include Resume or Profile for all partners and key employees (if needed form attached)					
Signed General Authorization Credit Form (see attached)					
Personal Tax Returns for the three prior years, including extensions and all supporting	2011				
	2010				
	2009				

Miscellaneous (as applicable)			Required	Received
Real Estate Purchase Agreement				
Copy of contract or bids for work to be done by contractor				
Plans and specifications and budgets				
Lease agreement if property current being leased				
Purhcase agreement if buying a business				
Copy of Franchise Agreement and Offering Circular if a Franchise				
Copy of any appraisal for property being financed				
Marketing materials, copy of web site, capabilites, etc.				

Other Items			Required	Received

COMMUNITY FACILITIES
REQUIREMENTS AND INFORMATION CHECKLIST

The following information must be provided[1] in order to compile a pre-application package for submission to the USDA:

Legal Name: _____ Dun & Bradstreet #: _____
    Address: _____
    _____ Employer ID #: _____
    County: _____

Congressional District – Applicant: _____ Project: _____

Proposed Project   Start Date: _____
                    End Date: _____

Funds Allocation:

Admin/Legal Expenses:	$_____	Land/Structures/Appraisals/etc:	$_____
Relocation Expenses:	$_____	Architectural/Engineering Fees:	$_____
Project Inspection Fees:	$_____	Site Work:	$_____
Demolition/Removal:	$_____	Construction:	$_____
Equipment:	$_____	Miscellaneous:	$_____
		TOTAL:	$_____

Pre-Application Information Required

___1.   Brief Description and History of the Project.
___2.   Historical (audits) for the last three years
___3.   Most current Interim Financial Statements
___4.   Projected Financial Statements
___5.   Applicant's organization documents (Articles of Incorporation, By-Laws, Operating Agreement) and a list of the Board of Directors/Officers.
___6.   Copy of any debt instrument for which the applicant is currently liable, if any.
___7.   Proposed sources and uses of funds.
___8.   Site Information (including location)
___9.   Evidence of Community Support from the effected local government body.
___10. Other information including appraisals, if available, and/or cost estimates.
___11. Any items used as Marketing Materials for the facility.

Please note: Additional information may be required to complete the "Pre-Application."

Information Required Upon Pre-Application Approval

___1.   Operating budget for current operating cycle.
___2.   Narrative statement describing organization's services, scope of operation, and geographical area served, including any proposed management agreements or leases.
___3.   Record of any pending litigation or regulatory action.
___4.   A "Certificate of Need" for facilities when required by State law.

Please note: A feasibility study will also be required if approved.
[1]Include N/A where information does not apply to project.

Appendix G

B&I AND CF SAMPLE TABLE OF CONTENTS

COMPANY TABLE OF CONTENTS

1. Forms
2. Business Plan/Project Summary
3. State Clearinghouse Comments or Recommendation
4. Feasibility Study
5. Architectural/Engineering Plans
6. Cost Estimates
7. Pending, Final Regulatory or Legal Action against Business
8. Certificate of Need
9. Guarantor's Financial Statements & 449-4 Statement of Personal History
10. Intergovernmental Review Clearance
11. Appraisals
12. Lender's Analysis
    a. Proposed Term Loan Agreement
    b. Interim Financial Statement
    c. 3 Years Historical Balance Sheets and Income Statements
    d. Proforma Balance Sheet

      e. 2 Years Projected YE Balance Sheets and Income Statements
      f. Borrower's Management
      g. Repayment Ability
      h. History of Debt Repayment
      i. Necessity for any Debt Refinancing
      j. Credit Reports
      k. Post Closing Tangible Equity Calculation
13. Other Materials
      a. Organizational Documents
      b. Corporate Tax Returns
      c. Personal Tax Returns
      d. Real Estate Legal Description
      e. Equipment List
      f. Marketing Material

COMPANY TABLE OF CONTENTS (CF PRE-APPLICATION)

BANK PROJECT SUMMARY LETTER

1. Application for Federal Assistance (Form SF-424)
2. Evidence of Significant Community Support
3. Historical Financial Statements (Audits)
4. Projected Financial Statements
5. Organizational Documents
6. Existing Debt Instruments
7. Proposed Use of Funds
8. Appraisals and Cost Estimates
9. Documentation of Lender Eligibility
10. Other Material

COMPANY
TABLE OF CONTENTS
(CF FULL APPLICATION)

1. Application for Loan and Guarantee (Form RD 3575-1)
2. Financial Feasibility Analysis/Report
3. Preliminary Architectural or Engineering Report
4. Cost Estimates
5. Intergovernmental Review and State Clearinghouse Comments or Recommendations
6. Request for Environmental Information (Form Rd 1940-20)
7. Standard Flood Hazard Determination (FEMA Form 81-93)
8. Regulatory Certifications (Certificate of Need, etc.)
9. Lender's Financial Analysis
10. Lender Certification
11. Project Summary (from Guaranteed Loan System)
12. Fund Analysis (from Guaranteed Loan System)
13. List of Board of Directors/Officers
14. Supporting Documentation to make an Eligibility Determination
15. Evidence of Significant Community Support
16. Affirmative Fair Housing Marketing Plan
17. Civil Rights Impact Analysis Certification (Form RD 2006-38)
18. Credit Report
19. Appraisal Report
20. Site Information
21. Lender's Commitment to Borrower
22. Environmental Assessment for Class I Action or Environmental Checklist for Category Exclusions

23. Findings of No Significant Impact
24. Clean Air/Water Pollution Compliance
25. Building Permits
26. Certification Regarding Debarment, Suspension and Other Responsibility Matters
27. Other Documents used by Lender that are Material to making a Credit Decision

Appendix H

GUIDELINE FOR FINANCIAL FEASIBILITY

(Guide 5)   RD Instruction 1942-A

FINANCIAL FEASIBILITY REPORT

I <u>General</u>.

The following may be used as a guide for the preparation of financial feasibility reports as required for Rural Development financed facilities. The guide contains minimal requirements and the report writer is expected to fully disclose and analyze all significant factors which will likely have a favorable or adverse effect on the financial success of the proposed facility.

A <u>Need for the facility</u>.

B <u>Existing facilities</u>.

Explain current capacities, rates or usage, activities, suitability for continued use, alternate usage, deficiencies in services, staffing, physical conditions, and any other pertinent information.

C <u>Proposed facility</u>.

1 Description of construction and renovation by component parts including capacity of each component part and physical limiting factors.

2 Explain and document the need for the facility. Include comments regarding the following:

  a Service area

  b Population trends

  c Similar facilities and services in the area

  d Usage trends

  e Community support

  f Regulatory agency approval

  g Economy in the service area

  h Analysis of staff and consultants

D <u>Financial information</u>.

1 Explain all assumptions underlying the expected demand, use, and projections of financial data, such as:

(1-15-79) SPECIAL PN

RD Instruction 1942-A
(Guide 5) (Page 2)

    a Changes in usage

    b All income and expense

    c Rate structure

    d Allowance for uncollectible accounts

    e Depreciation life and method

    f Description of long-term debts

2 Financial statements. The following financial statements must be prepared reflecting five years projections:

    a Balance sheet for all funds

    b Statement of income and expense

    c Statement of cash flow (cash receipts and disbursements)

    d Comparison data for facilities in service area (latest year only)

Appendix I

CONDITIONAL COMMITMENT

Form 4279-3
(Rev. 07-08)

UNITED STATES DEPARTMENT OF AGRICULTURE
RURAL DEVELOPMENT

CONDITIONAL COMMITMENT

FORM APPROVED
OMB NO. 0570-0017
OMB NO. 0570-0050

TO: Lender	Case No.
Lender's Address	State
Borrower	Principal Amount of Loan

From an examination of information supplied by the Lender and other relevant information, it appears that the transaction can properly be completed.

Therefore, the United States of America acting through the United States Department of Agriculture (USDA) hereby agrees that, in accordance with applicable provisions of the regulations, it will execute Form 4279-5, "Loan Note Guarantee," subject to the conditions and requirements specified in the regulations and herein.

The Loan Note Guarantee fee payable by the lender to USDA will be the amount as specified in the regulations on the date of this Conditional Commitment for Guarantee. The interest rate for the loan is _____ % 1/. If a variable rate is used, it must be tied to a base rate agreed to by the Lender and USDA which cannot change more often than quarterly (for Business and Industry) and must be published periodically in a financial publication specifically agreed to by the Lender and Borrower.

A Loan Note Guarantee will not be issued until the Lender certifies that there has been no adverse change in the Borrower's financial condition, nor any other adverse change in the borrower's condition, for any reason, during the period of time from USDA's issuance of this Conditional Commitment for Guarantee to issuance of the Loan Note Guarantee regardless of the cause or causes of the change and whether the cause or causes of the change were within the Lender's or Borrower's control. The Lender's certification must address all adverse changes and be supported by financial statements of the Borrower and its guarantors executed not more than 60 days before the time of certification. As used in this paragraph only, the term "Borrower" includes any parent, affiliate, or subsidiary of the Borrower.

In the event of the Government's failure to issue a guarantee in a situation where it is found to be in breach, the other party's remedy is limited to a suit for the guaranteed portion of principal and interest which ultimately remains unpaid.

This agreement becomes null and void unless the conditions are accepted by the Lender and Borrower within 60 days from the date of issuance by USDA.

Except as set out below, the purposes for which the loan funds will be used and the amounts to be used for such purposes are set out in the Application for Loan Guarantee. Once this instrument is executed and returned to USDA no major change of conditions or approved loan purpose as listed on the forms will be considered. Additional Conditions and Requirements including Source and Use of Funds: 2/

If the conditions set forth in this commitment are not met within _____ days from the date of this commitment, USDA reserves the right to discontinue the processing of the application and terminate its commitment. If USDA decides to terminate this commitment USDA will provide the Lender a written notice at least 14 days prior to termination. 3/

UNITED STATES OF AMERICA

By: _____

Typed or Printed Name: _____

Date: _____ _____
(Title)

According to the Paperwork Reduction Act of 1995, no persons are required to respond to a collection of information unless it displays a valid OMB control number. The valid OMB control number for this information collection is 0570-0017 and 0570-0050. The time required to complete this information is estimated to average 1.5 hours per response, including the time for reviewing instructions, searching existing data sources, gathering and maintaining the data needed, and completing and reviewing the collection of information.

ACCEPTANCE OF CONDITIONS

To: USDA 4/

The conditions of this Conditional Commitment for Guarantee including attachments are acceptable and the undersigned intends to proceed with the loan transaction and request issuance of a Loan Note Guarantee within _____ days.

_____
(Name of Lender)

Date: _____ By: _____
(Signature for Lender)

Date: _____   _____
(Signature for Borrower)

1/ Insert fixed interest rate or, if authorized by regulations, variable interest rate followed by a "V" and the appropriate loan subsidy rate, if applicable.

2/ Insert any additional conditions or requirements in this space or on an attachment referred to in this space; otherwise, insert "NONE".

3/ USDA will determine and insert the date by which conditions should be met.

4/ Return completed and signed copy of this form to USDA issuing office.

Appendix J

LOAN NOTE GUARANTEE

Form RD 4279-5
(Rev. 07-05)

7 CFR Part 4279
7 CFR Part 4280

UNITED STATES DEPARTMENT OF AGRICULTURE
RURAL DEVELOPMENT

LOAN NOTE GUARANTEE
(Business and Industry and Section 9006 Program)

State	County	Date of Note
Borrower		USDA Loan Identification Number
Lender		Lender's IRS Tax ID Number
Lender's Address		Principal Amount of Loan $

The guaranteed portion of the loan is $ _____ 0.00 which is _____ (_____ %) percent of loan principal. The principal amount of loan is evidenced by _____ notes (includes bonds as appropriate) described below. The guaranteed portion of each note is indicated below. This instrument is attached to note _____ in the face amount of $ _____ and is number _____ of _____

Lender's Identifying Number	Face Amount $	Percent of Total Face Amount %	Amount Guaranteed $
TOTAL	$ 0.00	100%	$ 0.00

In consideration of the making of the subject loan by the above named Lender, the United States of America, acting through the United States Department of Agriculture ("USDA"), pursuant to the Consolidated Farm and Rural Development Act (7 U.S.C. 1921 et seq), does hereby agree that in accordance with and subject to the conditions and requirements herein, it will pay to:

   A. Any Holder 100 percent of any loss sustained by such Holder on the guaranteed portion and on interest due on such portion.
   B. The Lender the lesser of paragraph 1 or 2 below:
      1. Any loss sustained by such Lender on the guaranteed portion including:
         a. Principal and interest indebtedness as evidenced by said notes or by assumption agreements, and
         b. Principal and interest indebtedness on secured protective advances for protection and preservation of collateral made with USDA's authorization, including but not limited to, advances for taxes, annual assessments, any ground rents, and hazard or flood insurance premiums affecting the collateral, or
      2. The guaranteed principal advanced to or assumed by the Borrower under said notes or assumption agreements and any interest due thereon.

        If USDA conducts the liquidation of the loan, loss occasioned to a Lender by accruing interest after the date USDA accepts responsibility for liquidation will not be covered by this Loan Note Guarantee. If Lender conducts the liquidation of the loan, accruing interest shall be covered by this Loan Note Guarantee to 30 days after liquidation of collateral when the lender conducts the liquidation expeditiously in accordance with the liquidation plan approved by USDA.

Definition of Holder.
    The Holder is the person or organization ("investor") other than the Lender who owns all or part of the guaranteed portion of the loan with no servicing responsibilities. Holders are prohibited from obtaining any parts of the guaranteed portion of the loan with proceeds from any obligation, the interest on which is excludable from income, under section 103 of the Internal Revenue Code of 1954, as amended (IRC). When the single note option is used and the Lender assigns a part of the guaranteed loan to an assignee, the assignee becomes a Holder only when USDA receives notice and the transaction is completed through use of Form 4279-6, "Assignment Guarantee Agreement."

Definition of Lender.
The Lender is the person or organization making and servicing the loan which is guaranteed under the provisions of 7 C.F.R. part 4279 or C.F.R. part 4280, subpart B, as applicable . The Lender is also the party requesting a loan guarantee.

CONDITIONS OF GUARANTEE

1. Loan Servicing.
Lender will be responsible for servicing the entire loan, and Lender will remain mortgagee and secured party of record not withstanding the fact that another party may hold a portion of the loan. When multiple notes are used to evidence a loan, Lender will structure repayments as provided in the loan agreement.

2. Priorities.
The entire loan will be secured by the same security with equal lien priority for the guaranteed and unguaranteed portions of the loan. The unguaranteed portion of the loan will not be paid first nor given any preference or priority over the guaranteed portion.

3. Full Faith and Credit.
The Loan Note Guarantee constitutes an obligation supported by the full faith and credit of the United States and is incontestable except for fraud or misrepresentation of which Lender or any Holder has actual knowledge at the time it became such Lender or Holder or which Lender or any Holder participates in or condones. The guarantee will be unenforceable to the extent that any loss is occasioned by a provision for interest on interest. In addition, the Loan Note Guarantee will be unenforceable by Lender to the extent any loss is occasioned by the violation of usury laws, negligent servicing, or failure to obtain the required security regardless of the time at which USDA acquires knowledge of the foregoing. Any losses occasioned will be unenforceable to the extent that loan funds are used for purposes other than those specifically approved by USDA in its Conditional Commitment for Guarantee. Negligent servicing is defined as the failure to perform those services which a reasonably prudent lender would perform in servicing (including liquidation) its own portfolio of loans that are not guaranteed. The term includes not only the concept of a failure to act but also not acting in a timely manner or acting in a manner contrary to the manner in which a reasonably prudent lender would act up to the time of loan maturity or until a final loss is paid.

4. Rights and Liabilities.
The guarantee and right to require purchase will be directly enforceable by Holder notwithstanding any fraud or misrepresentation by Lender or any unenforceability of this Loan Note Guarantee by Lender except for fraud or misrepresentation of which the Holder had actual knowledge at the time it became the Holder or in which the Holder participates or condones. Nothing contained herein will constitute any waiver by USDA of any rights it possesses against the Lender. Lender will be liable for and will promptly pay to USDA any payment made by USDA to Holder which, if such Lender had held the guaranteed portion of the loan, USDA would not be required to make.

5. Payments.
Lender will receive all payments of principal or interest, on account of the entire loan and will promptly remit to Holder its pro rata share thereof determined according to its respective interest in the loan, less only Lender's servicing fee.

6. Protective Advances.
Protective advances made by Lender pursuant to the regulations will be guaranteed against a percentage of loss to the same extent as provided in this Loan Note Guarantee notwithstanding the guaranteed portion of the loan that is held by another.

7. Repurchase by Lender.
The Lender has the option to repurchase the unpaid guaranteed portion of the loan from the Holder within 30 days of written demand by the Holder when: (a) the borrower is in default not less than 60 days on principal or interest due on the loan or (b) the Lender has failed to remit to the Holder its pro rata share of any payment made by the Borrower within 30 days of its receipt thereof. The repurchase by the Lender will be for an amount equal to the unpaid guaranteed portion of principal and accrued interest less the Lender's servicing fee. The Loan Note Guarantee will not cover the note interest to the Holder on the guaranteed loan accruing after 90 days from the date of the demand letter to the Lender requesting the repurchase. Holder will concurrently send a copy of demand to USDA. The Lender will accept an assignment without recourse from the Holder upon repurchase. The Lender is encouraged to repurchase the loan to facilitate the accounting for funds, resolve the problem, and to permit the borrower to cure the default, where reasonable. The Lender will notify the Holder and USDA of its decision.

8. USDA Purchase.
If Lender does not repurchase as provided by paragraph 7 USDA will purchase from Holder the unpaid principal balance of the guaranteed portion together with accrued interest to date of repurchase less Lender's servicing fee, within thirty (30) days after written demand to USDA from Holder. The Loan Note Guarantee will not cover the note interest to the Holder on the guaranteed loans accruing after 90 days from the date of the original demand letter of the Holder to the Lender requesting the repurchase. Such demand will include a copy of the written demand made upon the Lender. The Holder or its duly authorized agent will also include evidence of its right to require payment from USDA. Such evidence will consist of either the original of the Loan Note Guarantee properly endorsed to USDA or the original of the Assignment Guarantee Agreement properly assigned to USDA without recourse including all rights, title, and interest in the loan. USDA will be subrogated to all rights of Holder. The Holder will include in its demand the amount due including unpaid principal, unpaid interest to date of demand and interest subsequently accruing from date of demand to proposed payment date. Unless otherwise agreed to by USDA, such proposed payment will not be later than 30 days from the date of demand.

Appendix J: Loan Note Guarantee

The USDA will promptly notify the Lender of its receipt of the Holder's demand for payment. The Lender will promptly provide the USDA with the information necessary for USDA determination of the appropriate amount due the Holder. Any discrepancy between the amount claimed by the Holder and the information submitted by the Lender must be resolved before payment will be approved. USDA will notify both parties who must resolve the conflict before payment by USDA will be approved. Such conflict will suspend the running of the 30 day payment requirement. Upon receipt of the appropriate information, USDA will review the demand for verification. After receiving the demand, USDA will review the demand and remit the appropriate payment to the Holder.

9. <u>Lender's Obligations.</u>

Lender consents to the purchase by USDA and agrees to furnish on request by USDA a current statement certified by an appropriate authorized officer of the Lender of the unpaid principal and interest then owed by Borrowers on the loan and the amount then owed to any Holder. Lender agrees that any purchase by USDA does not change, alter or modify any of the Lender's obligations to USDA arising from said loan or guarantee nor does it waive any of USDA's rights against Lender, and that USDA will have the right to set-off against Lender all rights inuring to USDA as the Holder of this instrument against USDA's obligation to Lender under the Loan Note Guarantee.

10. <u>Repurchase by Lender for Servicing.</u>

If, in the opinion of the Lender, repurchase of the guaranteed portion of the loan is necessary to adequately service the loan, the Holder will sell the portion of the loan to the Lender for an amount equal to the unpaid principal and interest on such portion less Lender's servicing fee. The Loan Note Guarantee will not cover the note interest to the Holder on the guaranteed loan accruing after 90 days from the date of the demand letter of the Lender or USDA to the Holder requesting the Holder to tender its guaranteed portion.
    a. The Lender will not repurchase from the Holder for arbitrage purposes or other purposes to further its own financial gain.
    b. Any repurchase will only be made after the Lender obtains USDA written approval.
    c. If the Lender does not repurchase the portion from the Holder, USDA at its option may purchase such guaranteed portions for servicing purposes.

11. <u>Custody of Unguaranteed Portion.</u>

The Lender may retain, or sell the unguaranteed portion of the loan only through participation. Participation, as used in this instrument, means the sale of an interest in the loan wherein the Lender retains the note, collateral securing the note, and all responsibility for loan servicing and liquidation.

12. <u>When Guarantee Terminates.</u>

This Loan Note Guarantee will terminate automatically (a) upon full payment of the guaranteed loan; or (b) upon full payment of any loss obligation hereunder; or (c) upon written notice from the Lender to USDA that the guarantee will terminate 30 days after the date of notice, provided the Lender holds all of the guaranteed portion and the Loan Note Guarantee is returned to be cancelled by USDA.

13. <u>Settlement.</u>

The amount due under this instrument will be determined and paid as provided in the applicable USDA regulations in effect on the date of settlement unless such regulations are in direct conflict with this agreement.

14. <u>Notices.</u>

All notices will be initiated through the USDA _____

for _____ (State) with mailing address at the day of this instrument:

UNITED STATES OF AMERICA
Department of Agriculture

By:_____

Title:_____

_____
(Date)

Assumption Agreement by _____ Dated _____

Assumption Agreement by _____ Dated _____

Position 2

Form 4279-5 (07-05)

Appendix K

RD AN 4483
BUSINESS AND INDUSTRY GUARANTEED LOAN

AND

SECTION 9007
RURAL ENERGY FOR AMERICA PROGRAMS LENDER FINANCIAL ANALYSIS REQUIREMENTS

RD AN No. 4483 (4279-B, 4280-B, and 4287-B)
December 12, 2009

TO: State Directors, Rural Development

ATTN: Business Programs Directors

SUBJECT: Business and Industry Guaranteed Loan and Section 9007 Rural Energy for America Programs Lender Financial Analysis Requirements

PURPOSE/INTENDED OUTCOME:

This Administrative Notice (AN) is to provide guidance to lenders and State Office personnel on the minimum spread requirements and financial analysis standards that the lenders must perform to comply with RD Instruction 4287-B, section 4287.107(d), and Form RD 4279-4, "Lender's Agreement," paragraphs IV(c) (6) and (11). This AN delineates the minimum financial analysis that Business and Cooperative Programs believes a reasonably prudent lender would use for a performing loan. The Agency is also emphasizing the need and requirement for State Offices to maintain and track the servicing activity of nondelinquent problem loans in the Guaranteed Loan System (GLS). This guidance is also applicable to meeting the requirement contained in RD Instruction 4279-B, section 4279.161(b) (8).

The State Offices are requested to notify all lenders, in writing, that failure to obtain or analyze financial statements or properly service loans could be considered negligent servicing and the Loan Note Guarantee may be commensurately reduced as a result.

COMPARISON WITH PREVIOUS AN:

This AN replaces RD AN No. 4395 dated October 27, 2008, which expired on October 31, 2009.

EXPIRATION DATE:
December 31, 2010

FILING INSTRUCTIONS:
Preceding RD Instruction 4279-B, 4280-B, and 4287-B

Lender Financial Analysis Requirements 2

IMPLEMENTATION RESPONSIBILITIES:

The lender is responsible for obtaining and forwarding to the Agency the financial statements required by the Loan Agreement. The lender is responsible for providing the Agency with: (1) an analysis of the borrower's financial statements (including spreadsheets); and (2) a written trend analysis that compares the borrower's year-to-year historical financial information. The lender's analysis should also include a borrower ratio comparison to industry standards for similar size businesses. The lender's written analysis to the Agency must include the borrower's strengths, weaknesses, and extraordinary transactions. The analysis should identify any loan agreement violations and other indications of the financial condition of the borrower. The lender will submit the annual financial statements to the Agency, along with its spreadsheets and written analysis, within 120 days of the end of the borrower's fiscal year. Upon receipt, your office should spread and analyze the borrower's annual financial statements. A copy of the analysis will be filed in the case file.

It is the Agency's position that, at a minimum, a reasonably prudent lender would prepare the ratios identified on the attachment to this memorandum and provide this information to the Agency, along with its written summary of the analysis. Promptly obtaining and reviewing financial information from the borrower can reveal financial red flags that indicate problems the borrower may be experiencing and has not disclosed. These indicators provide guidance for adequately servicing the loan. A review of the financial statements assists the lender and State Office in determining the appropriate action that will maximize recovery to the Agency. It is important to note that every borrower is different. As such, we recognize economic conditions change, industry conditions are not constant, and public policy and community relations affect how lenders deal with problem loans.

A nonexclusive list of the lender's servicing responsibilities is contained in Form RD 4279-4, "Lender's Agreement," paragraph IV. The lender's servicing responsibilities include obtaining compliance with the loan covenants and getting the borrower's periodic financial statements, as required by the Loan Agreement.

We must increase our efforts to obtain financial statements, review lenders analyses, and provide follow-up to lenders on servicing deficiencies. Our files should be documented to show our attempts to obtain the required information.

For loan processing, it is the Agency's position that a reasonably prudent lender's financial analysis would consist of a complete, written analysis discussing: (1) adequacy of equity; (2) cashflow and repayment ability (including a cashflow analysis); (3) collateral; (4) borrower's management; (5) the borrower's history of credit and debt repayment; and (6) the necessity of any debt refinancing, (which should address the eligibility criteria outlined in RD Instruction 4279-B, section 4279.113(r)). The lender's analysis must also include spreadsheets of the

Lender Financial Analysis Requirements 3

balance sheets and income statements for 3 historical years and 2 projected years as well as a pro forma balance sheet at loan closing that reflects the post-closing status. These spreadsheets should be common-sized and the figures compared to industry standards.

In addition, the State Office should place increased emphasis on maintaining the GLS in a current status on all Business and Industry (B&I) guaranteed loans, which includes reporting all nondelinquent problem loans into GLS. The B&I Guaranteed Loan Program is growing, and it is important that the Agency properly monitor guaranteed lenders to minimize potential losses to the Government. As part of the Business and Cooperative Programs Assessment Reviews, the National Office has implemented an observation and comparison of nondelinquent problem loans serviced by the State Office and the numbers reported in the GLS. Periodically, you may also be asked to submit your GLS reports of nondelinquent problem loans to the National Office for spot reviews.

In accordance with RD Instruction 4280-B, section 4280.152(a), all Section 9007 Rural Energy for America guaranteed loans are to be serviced in accordance with RD Instruction 4287-B, section 4287.107.

If you have any questions, please contact the B&I Division, Servicing Branch, at (202) 690-4103.

(Signed by Judith A. Canales)

JUDITH A. CANALES
Administrator
Business and Cooperative Programs

Attachment

Attachment

FINANCIAL STATEMENT ANALYSIS

At a minimum, the lender's financial analysis should include, but is not limited to, the following:

1. **Current Ratio**: Measures the ability of a company to pay its currently maturing obligations on a timely basis. It shows the amount of protection provided by a company's current assets relative to its current liabilities.

   Total current assets
   Total current liabilities

2. **Quick Ratio**: Expresses the degree to which current liabilities of a company are covered by the most liquid current assets. This acid test ratio is a more stringent measure of liquidity than the current ratio, because the quick ratio includes only the most liquid current assets or those that can be quickly converted to cash at amounts close to their book value.

   Cash + Accounts receivable (trade) + Marketable securities
   Total current liabilities

3. **Days Accounts Receivable Ratio**: Expresses the average time in days that receivables are outstanding. The collection period varies greatly for different types of companies and it is important to make comparisons with similar companies or to look at trends over time.

   365
   Net sales/Accounts receivable

4. **Days Inventory Ratio**: Measures the company purchasing, selling, and manufacturing efficiency, but is meaningful only in relation to the company's past performance and the performance of similar companies in the same industry.

   365
   Cost of goods sold/Inventory

5. **Debt-to-Worth Ratio**: Provides an indication of how well the investment of the shareholder in the company protects a creditor debt. It also measures how much the shareholders have at risk versus how much the creditors have at risk and, thus, the strength of the company capital structure.

   Total liabilities
   Tangible net worth

6. **Times-Interest-Earned Ratio**: Measures what proportion of the company earnings is needed to pay interest on its debt. A ratio of 1 is almost mandatory, since a lower ratio would indicate company earnings are insufficient to cover the interest on its debt.

   Earnings before taxes + Interest expense
   Interest expense

7. **Debt Service Coverage Ratio**: Measures the proportion of a company's net profit and noncash expenses that will be needed to pay the principal portion of long-term debt in the coming year.

   Net profit + Depreciation + Other non-cash charges
   Current maturities of long-term debt

8. **Return-On-Sales Ratio (or Net Profit Margin)**: Measures the extent to which revenues of a company exceeds all its expenses, that is, how much profit the company earns on each dollar of sales.

   Profits before taxes
   Net sales

9. **Return-on-Assets**: Measures the profitability of a company in terms of how efficiently it uses its assets.

   Profit before taxes
   Total assets

10. **Return-on-Equity Ratio**: A high return, normally associated with effective management, could indicate an under-capitalized firm. A low return, usually an indicator of inefficient management performance, could reflect a highly capitalized, conservatively operated business.

    Profit before taxes
    Tangible net worth

ABOUT THE AUTHOR

Greg O'Donnell grew up in Joplin, Missouri, and started his life as an entrepreneur in the fourth grade, selling and delivering the *TV Guide* every week after school. He delivered twenty-five to thirty guides per week, netting approximately a nickel a copy, which was not bad money for the late 1950s.

In his early teens, Greg moved on to mowing lawns. In high school he started working at an auto parts supply store and continued working there to support himself through college "the hard way," working as many hours as possible to pay for college tuition and all the extras that contributed to his unique college experience.

After graduating from Missouri Southern State University in 1974, Greg moved to Tulsa, Oklahoma, where he began work in a regional public accounting firm that went through a series of mergers and eventually became Peat Marwick International. In 1976 he became a Certified Public Accountant and joined Cities Service Oil Company, becoming the company's youngest-ever manager of budget and reporting. Greg has held a number of positions through the years, ranging from controller to CFO to vice president of finance, but in all those positions he found he was always searching for funding for expansions or acquisitions. That is when Greg discovered the guaranteed loan programs that he describes in this book.

Today Greg owns five companies, all centered on guaranteed lending in one way or another.

His soon-to-be-released *Everything Your Banker Knows about Your Business: What Every Business Owner Needs to Know Before He Asks His Banker for Money* offers an inexpensive lesson and wake-up call for all business owners who are considering asking their banker for money.

In the course of the past eighteen years, Greg has originated and packaged more than $350 million in guaranteed loans, all through referral and repeat business. He is known nationally as the leading authority on USDA Lending but most just call him the "USDA GURU."

Greg recently added bank coaching to his company under the name of The USDA Loan Experts, which is a division of Business Finance & Development (BF&D). In this program, Greg coaches bankers through the entire process—from marketing, originating, and packaging to closing and servicing USDA guaranteed loans, resulting in a significant positive effect on each bank's bottom line.

Greg has been married for twenty-three years and has, with his wife, raised two sons—one graduated from the Air Force Academy and served as a fighter pilot for ten years and the other is an accomplished musician who won a world championship playing with the Blue Devils Drum and Bugle Corps, in Concord, California.

Greg currently works with his wife, B.J., from his office in Tulsa, Oklahoma.